Andreas Uebele Signage Systems & Information Graphics

A Professional Sourcebook

With over 500 illustrations in colour and black and white

Thames & Hudson

Foreword During my student days I worked as a temp in an architectural firm, where one of my first assignments was to design some signs and an information board. I didn't really see the point as architecture ought to be self-explanatory, but that was what the architect wanted me to do. By the evening, everything was ready. The beautifully justified Helvetica font and grey level looked great and I felt very pleased with myself. But that same evening I underwent a crash course in typography, during which my beloved Helvetica was taken apart. The grey tone was not the fail-safe I had thought, and my design was pronounced a total failure. The following morning, I set to work again, and this time drew down upon myself the criticism of the entire bureau. It's not easy to stand at the crossroads between architecture and graphic design.

One of those who can move with supreme skill from one to the other, displaying absolute mastery of both, is Professor Andreas Uebele. He studied architecture, urban development and graphic design, and currently teaches concepts and design in the Communications Department at the Fachhochschule in Düsseldorf. This book offers a complete guide to the basics of signage system design. With the aid of outstanding examples and penetrating analysis, Professor Uebele leads us expertly through the jungle of options, focusing on wayfinding and emphasizing the need for restraint but, at the same time, for absolute clarity in the system. The latter should ideally prevent people from getting lost and also create a visual identity. Very little has been published about signage systems, and so we thank Andreas Uebele with all our hearts for his time, expertise, diligent research and thoroughness. The result is a truly wonderful book.

Karin Schmidt-Friderichs

Introduction No handbook and no instruction manual can do away with the necessity to think for oneself. And every time a rule is broken, it marks a step in the direction of good design.

The first part of this book explains the 'rules' one ought to know before planning a signage system. Rules are there to be broken, but it is a very good idea to know what they are before you break them. Of course, in a field such as signage, where the rules are largely unwritten, this is easier said than done. The theoretical section of this book, therefore, focuses on ideas relating to the design parameters that are important to the planning process, drawing on many years of practical experience. They cover fonts and colours that might be appropriate for some cases but not for others, and offer some insight into arrows and pictograms. General 'rules' or guidelines have been marked in red and are found in the top corners of the relevant pages. The projects described in the theoretical section are mainly those carried out by our own firm, and you will find further information on these projects at the end of the book. When the examples stem from other companies, the source is always given. All the texts accompanying these projects have been written by the firms that planned them.

The second part of this book is a step-by-step guide to a possible planning process, which should be of some assistance to beginners. When designing my very first signage system – which turned out to be an unexpectedly major task – I was only too grateful for whatever help I could get. The architect had given me, not entirely for altruistic reasons, the details of a signage system designed by some of his colleagues for another project, all in the strictest confidence, of course. Although I felt guilty about it, I eagerly accepted, and now with this book I hope to atone in some degree for my 'crime'.

The third chapter profiles projects that can be held up as examples of first-class design. The selection has primarily been based on originality.

A signage system can be more than just a sign. It can give a place its identity, and figures and lettering can be an attractive adornment in themselves if properly designed. No one questions the necessity of signage systems when a place or event involves directing large numbers of people, and it's taken for granted that hospitals, airports, trade fairs and the like need wayfinding methods. The necessity is less obvious in some other spheres, but no matter what the context, any system of signs is liable to be both confusing and obtrusive if its communicatory function is not professionally planned and designed. Shortcomings will stand out like a sore thumb! It is much better to work with communications designers right from the outset, as you will see from the projects described here. In all the best examples, the graphic elements blend in perfectly with the architecture.

This book aims to encourage architects to tackle wayfinding in much the same way as they view the choice of, say, light switches and door handles – as an individual detail that contributes to the overall effect of the whole. It will also appeal to interior designers and others who may be struggling to come to terms with such systems, but above all it is for communications designers who appreciate the need for good planning in wayfinding.

Andreas Uebele

Terminology

Terminology

'Finding the way is not a gift or an innate ability that one either has or does not have. It is a precondition for life itself. Our approach to environments of whatever kind is part of our existence. Living with our respective ways of navigating is a basic premise for our liberty and our self-confidence. Knowing where I am, my location, is the precondition for knowing where I have to go, wherever it may be.'
Otl Aicher

Signage Systems, Wayfinding Systems and Directional Systems

A good rule would be to talk of wayfinding systems instead of directional systems.

You are unlikely to find the terms 'signage systems', 'wayfinding systems' or 'directional systems' in the dictionary. These are concepts that are as new as the subject itself. Equally new is the whole concept of systematic design that blends together all the technical and functional requirements of a project, although the actual task of showing people the way is as old as humankind. The arrow, for example, is an age-old sign, and in ancient times piles of stones used to point the way at crossroads.

One important factor is the number of people involved and the amount of time available. Giving clear information as quickly as possible to large crowds seems a relatively modern concern, although presumably Roman arenas were cleared pretty quickly, and it would be interesting to know how they did it. At a hospital, airport or trade fair, visitors want to get to the right area as quickly as possible but are often confronted with a bewildering choice of A, B, C etc. Just as people have to be directed through buildings and streets, they also need efficient systems to guide them at transport terminals. A clearly designed system of timetables and destinations is indispensable. One of the very first designs to have used a combination of words and graphics was the map of the London Underground, originally conceived by Harry Beck in 1931.

Displays of train and flight times are just as much informational systems as the navigational instruments of a car, offering data and directions. A university timetable of lectures may also indicate the rooms where lectures take place. However, we shall not be dealing with such informational systems in this book, where the main focus will be on spatial orientation.

Signage systems You can tell a company by its graphics. If a building bears the firm's font, or is adorned with the appropriate signs and lettering, it sends out a friendly signal that accomplishes a great

Signage system at Herz-Jesu-Kirche, Völklingen-Ludweiler. The lettering on the church door adds visual identity. See also page 34.

deal more than simply giving the address. The concept of such systems is described by the French as *signalétique*, which has been adopted by the Swiss and the Germans as *Signaletik*, emphasizing the active signal more than the sign. This term denotes actions – indication, suggestion, identification, recognition – in contrast to the less dynamic wayfinding system. In English less of a distinction is made between these different systems, which are usually all bracketed together under 'signage'.

Wayfinding systems Anton Stankowski objects to the very concept of directional systems, since they degrade the observer to the level of a passive, totally dependent object being led through a building. Such 'direction' differs from the passivity of wayfinding aids, as it is up to you whether you take advantage of the latter. And if we look a little more closely at what lies behind these linguistic terms, the design too is different. Active direction imposes itself intrusively on the foreground, and is an end in itself.

It entails leadership, domination, irresistible authority. A wayfinding system is polite and restrained, and may hide itself away when it is not needed. If you were not looking for it, you could easily miss it.

Directional systems This is not such an appealing term. The idea of being guided, informed and helped is far more pleasant and gentle than the domineering 'direct', or being actively led. A leader can also mislead, as many a nation has discovered to its cost.

9

'Typography and architecture intersect. Every building has some kind of writing. Houses bear signs. In important buildings, stonemasons and architects leave their signatures on stones. House numbers can be decorative or intrusive, while the doorbell and the letterbox may serve as visiting cards. The written word is an accompaniment to the erected stone, and well-chosen typography enriches the architecture. It can work with the building, but it can also work against it. Whether unusual or discreet, hard or soft, the lettering should always be integral to the architecture, its ally rather than its enemy.'

Andreas Uebele

1.1 Eye Level

The top of the sign is 145 cm above floor level, and is 4 cm from the frame, to ensure that the shadow from the door doesn't fall on the sign, which fits in with the surface and is visually integrated into it.

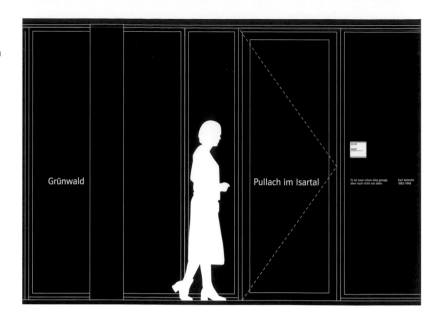

One absurd 'golden rule' states that an eye level of 163 cm is the ideal height for conveying information. As a general principle, all rules should be questioned, and especially this one. No one really knows where it came from. It may be the average eye level in Europe, but it is likely to have been based on an exercise in arithmetic rather than any genuine form of experiment. Whatever its origin, the measurement of 163 cm divides walls into unbalanced proportions, which is far from ideal. It is better to relate graphics or directions to the horizontal angles of the structure, i.e. where the ceiling meets the wall, or the wall meets the floor, as the information will then be visually more prominent and will be better integrated with the rest of the building. When graphics are placed roughly in the centre of a wall, they tend to be swamped.

When we are standing upright, looking straight ahead, it is possible that our eyes cover a field whose average height is 163 cm above the ground. However, we do not normally walk in a strictly perpendicular manner – our heads tilt slightly forward, and our eyes therefore drop. This is another reason why information should not be placed at eye level. A good height for the upper edge of a sign on a door, for example, would be 145 cm.

Information at a trade fair or an airport needs to be placed high up, where it can be read above people's heads. The same applies to signposts for lorry drivers, who are seated much higher than motorists. The information must be at such a height that it is not concealed by parked cars or pedestrians.

Wayfinding system at the Fachhochschule in Osnabrück. This system makes use of the human eye's natural angle of vision. From a distance of about 10 m, the viewer can perceive the writing on the ceiling without having to raise his head unnaturally. See also pages 26, 80 and 202–7.

The height at which information is displayed depends on the environment. Bus and lorry drivers, pedestrians and motorists read from different viewpoints.

Wayfinding system at the Neue Messe, Stuttgart. Pylon signs give directions to the car parks and exhibition halls etc. See also pages 29, 42–47, 62–63, 67, 88–89, 93, 102–103 and 127.

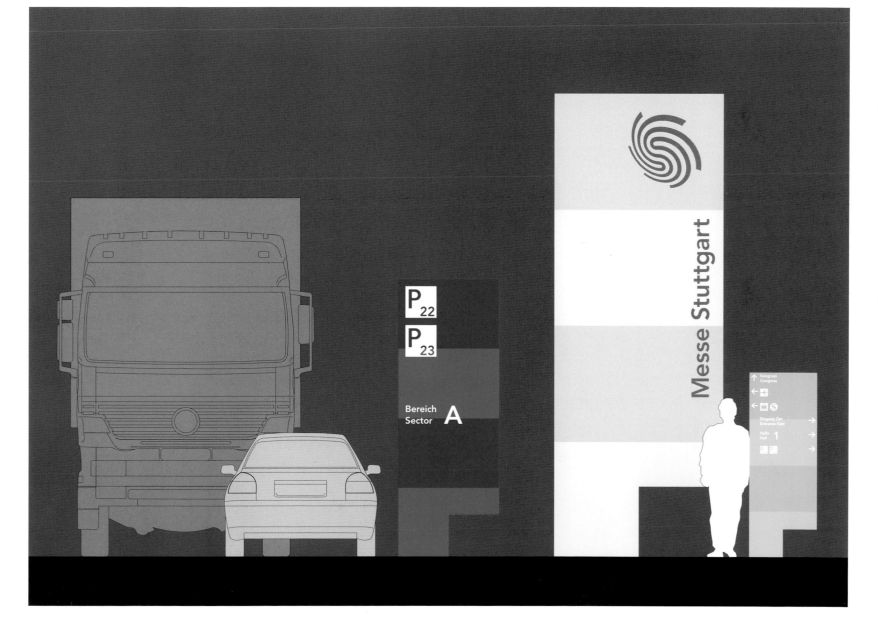

1.2 Light

Wayfinding system at the Bollwerk Service Centre, Landesbank Baden-Württemberg. White backgrounds can be dazzling. During the day, natural light hits the white wall, which makes the black (transfer tape) letters stand out. At night, when the white wall becomes dark, the white lettering stands out.

Illuminated signs can be beautiful and, in certain environments, essential. They are indispensable in airports, for example, where the surroundings can be visually overwhelming. There are various types of illuminated displays available on the market, but nearly all of them are unsatisfactory. One disadvantage is the cost. Clients are generally dependent on one particular supplier once the initial order has been made, leaving them vulnerable to price hikes should they come back for repeat orders. If a commission requires the development of a special extrusion press, this will drive prices up still further. The client will then, however, be the sole owner of this design, and if he wishes to extend or vary it, he can go on the open market to different suppliers for more competitive quotes.

The same applies to all in-house designs, where manufacture is not restricted to one company. If a design is developed for a particular project, it is essential to produce simple models in order to test the lighting effects before building a prototype.

Light can lead us, but such installations require maintenance and an architect or any other client must be fully aware of what he is taking on. Light can also dazzle. For the wayfinding system used at the Cologne/Bonn Airport (pages 138–43), the designers decided to use a matt background in order to keep reflections to a minimum, as this can seriously reduce legibility. However, in notoriously dingy places, such as underground car parks, lettering can be displayed on phosphorescent or reflective material.

This internally illuminated sign at the High Performance Computer Centre, Stuttgart University, acts as a light installation and is a focal point. The gold lettering matches the gold ceiling. See also pages 35 and 107.

Generally, white (or light-coloured) lettering on glass surfaces is easier to read than black. Glass acts like a mirror, reflecting the surroundings.

1.2　Light

If a sign is made of glass or acrylic plastic with a printed colour background, it may seem sensible to use replaceable white transfer tape for the letters. However, this has one serious disadvantage: the lettering throws a definite shadow onto the background. The thickness of the glass causes distortion, which is ugly and reduces legibility.

Wayfinding system at Stuttgart Airport. Information panels are backlit, against the daylight. Here the design minimizes the dazzling effect.
• The unusually large formats give the eye a comfortable, dark background to shut out the brightness of the daylight.

• The two colours of the lettering, white and black, stand out vividly against their respective backgrounds.
• The thickness of the lettering makes it stand out against the background surface.

Signage Design

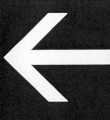

CHECK-IN 601–699

**ANKUNFT 6
ARRIVAL 6**

Wayfinding system, Stuttgart Airport, illuminated sign, prototype (see also pages 32–33, 52-53, 65, 82–83, 96–97, 113 and 123).

In 1916, Edward Johnston designed the Johnston font for the London Underground, in collaboration with Eric Gill. This font is a cross between serif and sans serif. The wayfinding system in the London Underground is both effective and attractive, and the lettering substantially adds to its brand identity.

A condensed font with large apertures lends itself well to wayfinding systems, as it takes up less space. Ideally it should have a high x-height, as this reinforces its legibility. All fonts should have the necessary variety of styles (bold, italic, etc), although there are exceptions to this rule that are equally successful. For the Paris Metro, only one style of the Métro font was used.

There are many good books on fonts, some of which are listed in the bibliography on page 334. Most of what Jan Tschichold wrote on the subject remains just as applicable today, with very few exceptions. In order to plan a signage system, a good designer must know the rules of font design, so that he can confidently apply and adapt. Texts for a wayfinding system must be designed with as much care as for any other task.

In the late 1960s, Adrian Frutiger was faced with the challenge of designing a wayfinding system at the new Charles de Gaulle Airport in Roissy, Paris. The Frutiger font was his answer, setting the benchmark for successful lettering in signage. The letters are legible, attractive and can be produced in a variety of subtly different styles. In principle, they could be used for any aspect of a wayfinding system and would do the job perfectly.

As far as Adrian Frutiger was concerned, however, each situation or set of circumstances was unique in itself. He designed an all-caps font called Métro for the Paris underground system (see 2, opposite), putting forward a simple but convincing argument for his use of upper case: the different names of the stations are striking enough in themselves, easily distinguishable, and therefore do not need any differentiation through upper and lower case.

Lettering must fit the architectural context. A modern-looking Frutiger font would seem thoroughly out of place in a baroque building.

Exit
Ausgang
Sortie

(1) Frutiger 65 Bold, designed in 1976 by Adrian Frutiger for the wayfinding system at the Charles de Gaulle Airport.
(2) Métro Regular, also designed by Frutiger for the Paris Metro. Sadly this font, which helped to give the Paris Metro its identity, has recently been abandoned.

(3) In 2000, Frutiger was reworked by the Linotype Library, in collaboration with Adrian Frutiger himself, into Frutiger Next. The black outline is in Frutiger Next Medium, and the grey is in Frutiger 55 Roman.

(4) The Astra-Frutiger (Adrian Frutiger, 2002) is used on Swiss motorways in two styles: Autobahn (top) and Standard (bottom). The large apertures and wide spacing between the letters improve legibility from a distance and when on the move.

EXIT
AUSGANG
SORTIE

Ausfahrt
Ausfahrt

Exit
Ausgang
Sortie

19

1.3 Fonts
Comparing Fonts

Below: When Frutiger Bold Condensed (top) and Syntax Bold (bottom) are set one above the other, the former is much easier on the eye. This distinction is particularly noticeable in the terminals of the 'A' (both upper case and lower case) and the 'C', as well as the commas. Straight vertical and horizontal terminals suit the orthogonal structures of signs.

Opposite: These words have been ordered according to the width of their characters. This is an important factor to take into consideration in wayfinding design, where fonts that take up the least space are preferred. The fonts shown here have large apertures and are easily legible.

The fonts shown opposite are suitable for wayfinding systems. Of course there are others that may work just as well, but these ones have one thing in common: they are all plain and functional, which enables them to blend in with the architectural features of their surroundings. They are all bold, as experience has taught us that bold lettering has more impact and can stand out against coloured backgrounds in visually 'loud' surroundings. As always, however, the exception may prove the rule, and a fine face with thin strokes may also have its place.

Some fonts have been successfully designed for particular purposes. The GST Polo is a striking example of an outstandingly original font for corporate design. The same could be said of Futura, Gill Sans and Syntax. In wayfinding systems, individual letters are shown in a very large point size ('Gate A', for example). A typeface that has been specifically designed for signage will not necessarily work on a reduced scale – in a book, for example – and vice versa.

Gate A, B, C

Frutiger 67 Bold Condensed,
Adrian Frutiger, 1976

Gate A, B, C

Syntax Bold,
Hans Eduard Meyer, 1969

Linotype Univers Condensed Medium	**Signage Systems**
Frutiger 65 Medium Condensed	Signage Systems
Helvetica Neue 67 Condensed Medium	**Signage Systems**
Vectora 75 Bold	**Signage Systems**
News Gothic Bold	**Signage Systems**
Frutiger Next Bold	**Signage Systems**
FF DIN Bold	**Signage Systems**
Avenir Next Demi	Signage Systems
Avenir 85 Heavy	**Signage Systems**
Corporate S Bold	**Signage Systems**
Frutiger 65 Bold	**Signage Systems**
Interstate Bold	**Signage Systems**
Akzidenz Grotesk Bold	**Signage Systems**
Helvetica Neue 75 Bold	**Signage Systems**
Linotype Univers Basic Bold	**Signage Systems**

The width of the letters that make up a word (see page 21) is a key consideration, but not the only one. Equally important are apertures and x-height, which are integral to legibility.

Opposite: Although these are great fonts, they are unsuitable for wayfinding systems, with their lobes, tails and idiosyncratic shapes. The circular 'O' in Futura could easily be confused with a zero, and the lower-case 't' looks like a grave cross.

1
Hannover
Vectora 75 Bold

2
Hannover
News Gothic Bold

3

Hannover
Vectora 75 Bold (black),
News Gothic Bold (grey)

4
Hannover
Vectora 75 Bold (black),
News Gothic Bold (grey)

5
Hannover
Vectora 75 Bold (black),
News Gothic Bold (grey)

Syntax Bold,
Hans Eduard Meyer,
1969

Polo 22k Semibold,
Georg Salden, 1976

Futura T Bold,
Paul Renner, 1928

Any comparison between fonts depends on different criteria. Naturally, the width of the letters is not the only important factor, as you can see clearly from the illustrations opposite. The two fonts Vectora and News Gothic were set in the same size (24 pt) in Adobe Illustrator (ills 1 & 2). The cap height of the News Gothic is 2% greater than the Vectora (ill. 3), even though they are in the same font size. In ill. 4, this has been corrected. The News Gothic has been reduced to make the capital 'H' the same size in both fonts. In the next step (ill. 5), the Vectora has been reduced so that the x-height is exactly the same as that of the News Gothic. Using a similar amount of space, the Vectora can be reduced by 14% without affecting its legibility. This example shows that readability is mainly dependent on the shape of the smaller letters. Vectora would therefore be recommended where several lines have to be fitted into a small space. Fonts with a large x-height remain easy to read in smaller sizes.

The fonts on page 21 are neutral and discreet, which is why they work so well in wayfinding systems, but there are many other fonts that could potentially disorientate, including the three examples illustrated above. Syntax, Polo and Futura would all be effective and even attractive on a smaller scale in certain contexts, but their ornate features make them unsuitable for large-scale projects – the swinging lobe and tail in the first and second 'g' respectively, for example, and the sloping ends of each stroke in the 'K'.

Gerard Unger's Capitolium, used in the wayfinding system for the millennium celebrations in Rome.

ABCDEFGHIJKLMNOPQRSTUVWXYZÆŒ
abcdefghijklmnopqrstuvwxyzßœœ
0123456789 (.,-:;)

ABCDEFGHIJKLMNOPQRSTUVWXYZÆŒ
abcdefghijklmnopqrstuvwxyzßæœ
0123456789 (.,-:;)

There are certain basic criteria for choosing a font. Does it fit in with the image of the company and/ or the project? Is it too ornate? Serif fonts do not work as well in signage systems as their sans serif counterparts, primarily because such purely functional systems need to be as straightforward and direct as possible. Of course everyone is familiar with the argument that a reading font is easier on the eye in running texts, and this may well be true. But in the context of signage systems, this argument is irrelevant as there is usually very little text. Naturally, there's nothing to stop you from choosing a reading font – for example Times, which is attractive, unpretentious and legible. The problem lies in its formal characteristics. In a book, letters accumulate into a body of text, where the overall form is of little importance. They are tiny elements in relation to the page, where the rectangular spread of letters corresponds to the shape of the book.

In a wayfinding system, this relationship is reversed. A handful of large letters stand on a small and restricted surface. The individual forms of the letters are directly connected to that surface and its restrictive borders, which for the most part tend to be rectangular, sharply defined and simple. These characteristics respond more effectively to a font with similar formal qualities – i.e. sans serif, straight and solid. The stems and strokes of serif characters tend to be tapered, clashing against the stiff rectangles of regular signs.

Gerard Unger successfully broke this rule when he designed the serif font Capitolium, which was used for the wayfinding system at Rome's millennium celebrations. In a city with such a rich architectural history, a sans serif font would, in fact, have seemed thoroughly out of place.

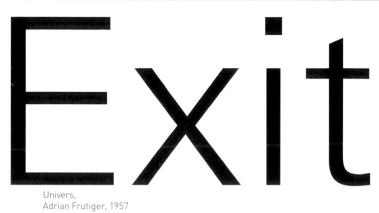

Univers,
Adrian Frutiger, 1957

Compare Univers (sans serif) with Times (serif): the former distracts the eye far less than the latter. Most of the angles in Univers are rectangular, and are therefore far more suited to orthogonal signs.

The strokes in Univers are more or less equal, whereas in Times their thickness varies, and there are curves and many more angles competing for our attention.

Sans serif fonts are generally more suitable than serifs in wayfinding systems.

Times,
Stanley Morrison, 1932

In Univers, the white areas create three rectangles. The form of these surfaces mirrors the shape of a rectangular sign.

In Times, the white areas create three irregular forms, which would be incongruous on a rectangular sign.

Capitolium,
Gerard Unger, 1998

25

1.3 Fonts
Choice of Font

In addition to the strict typographical criteria to which a font must conform if it is to be considered for a wayfinding system (e.g. legibility and available space), there is another important aspect to consider. Will the character of the font fit in with the architectural surroundings? And how exactly can you judge its suitability? This can be tested visually to some extent – if lettering becomes blurred up close, for example, or is difficult to read from certain standpoints, then it is unsuitable. The examples shown here are legible from all angles, demonstrating just why the particular font has been chosen.

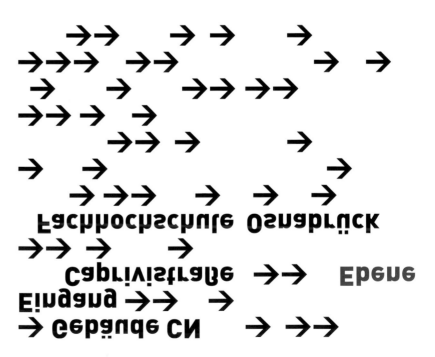

Wayfinding system at the Paulusstift in Stuttgart. The bold style of Adrian Frutiger's soft, rounded Avenir font counters the rigidity of the layout. The curved shape of the letters and the superscript dots and umlauts echo the circles in the background.

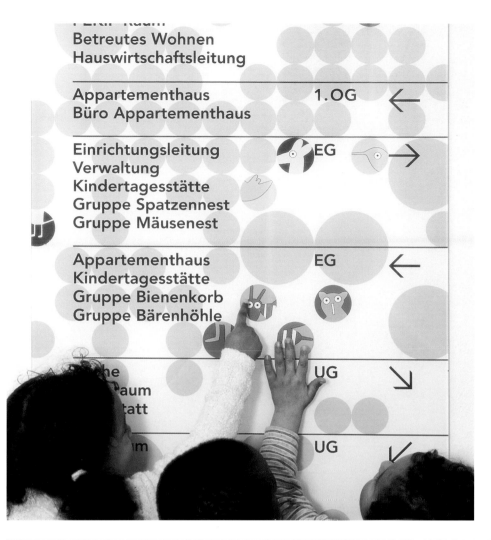

Wayfinding system at the Sophie Scholl School. There could be only one font for this project: Rotis, designed by Otl Aicher, who had close ties with the Scholls (he was married to Sophie's sister). Sophie was a heroine of the German Resistance.

1.3 Fonts
Choice of Font

Wayfinding system at the Berufschul-zentrum in Bitterfeld. The choice of FF DIN reflects the strict rules and high standards associated with vocational training at such institutions. This was designed in 1995 by Albert-Jan Pool and is a variation on the German DIN font.

Contribution to Designers Saturday in Stuttgart. Cardboard letters in Max Miedinger's Helvetica (1957) were set up outside the window of a furniture shop selling USM Haller, Knoll International and vitra.

The display reads: 'How can I furnish my text? There are a handful of comfortable and beautiful types. Some came into being long ago, others today. We don't need any more.'

Wayfinding system at the Neue Messe, Stuttgart. This Avenir font by Adrian Frutiger (1988) has basic geometrical forms but was designed by hand. Its name is a reference to its precursor, Paul Renner's Futura (1928).

The rounded characters of Avenir stand out against the rectangular bands running horizontally across the background. A straighter font like Frutiger, Helvetica or Univers would have complemented these bands, but the latter were specifically designed as a background pattern to the lettering.

1.3 Fonts
Choice of Font

Below right:
Wayfinding system
for Elektrotechnische
Institute II, Stuttgart
University. Here, in
choosing the font, the
designer has attached
more importance
to creating the right
ambience than any
practical, functional
criteria.

The austere charm
of Helvetica blends in
well with the mix of
red, purple, dark
green and grey.
See also page 66.

Above: Wayfinding
system at Kronen
Carré in Stuttgart.
The metal inlays in the
floor of the foyer give
the main directions.
The information is
shown in the Basic
Light and Basic
Medium styles of
Linotype Univers.

Adrian Frutiger
reworked his Univers
font into Linotype
Univers in 1998.
The clear, solid
form of Univers
suits the rhythmically
orthogonal pattern of
the sandstone slabs.
See also pages 79
and 101.

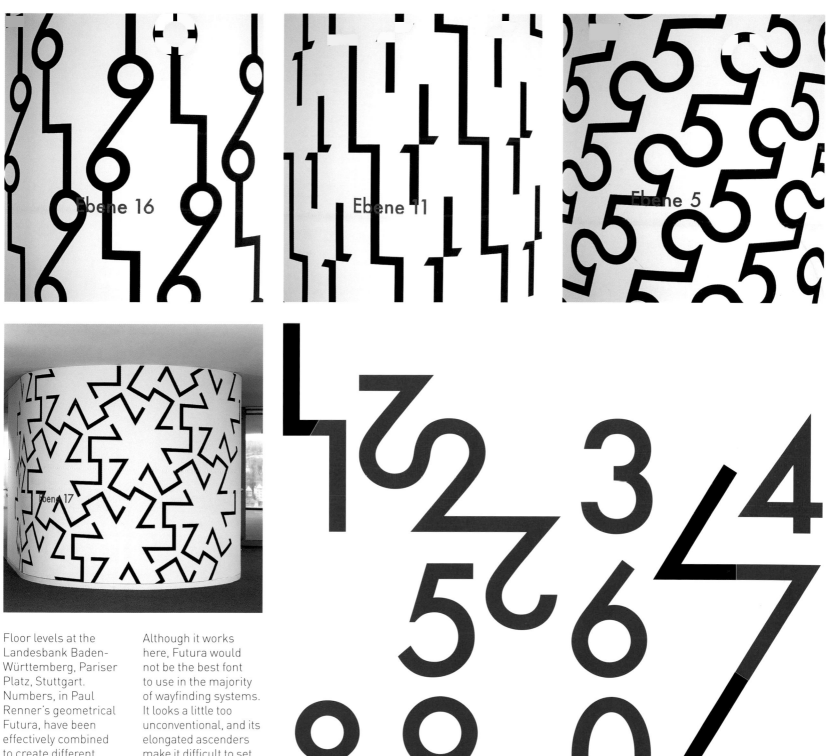

Floor levels at the Landesbank Baden-Württemberg, Pariser Platz, Stuttgart. Numbers, in Paul Renner's geometrical Futura, have been effectively combined to create different patterns.

Although it works here, Futura would not be the best font to use in the majority of wayfinding systems. It looks a little too unconventional, and its elongated ascenders make it difficult to set letters close together, taking up more space. See also page 95.

1.3 Fonts
Choice of Font

Wayfinding system at Stuttgart Airport. This project required an efficient, self-contained system. The font is a strong visual marker and contributes to the brand equity, like a logo or trademark. Helvetica, which was in use at the time, is ideal for this purpose and fully deserves its popularity.

In this particular wayfinding system, however, only capitals were used, and it was therefore decided that Interstate would be more suitable than Helvetica (see opposite).

The design of the wayfinding system at Stuttgart Airport is based on a few very simple ideas: a large and eye-catching format, an effective colour scheme of red, black and white, and unusual typography. In order to keep the effect of the coloured surfaces as neutral as possible, only capital letters were used.

As there are just a few short words displayed, the caps do not affect legibility. Words like 'Exit', 'Gate' and 'Departure' are easily distinguishable from one another.

Check-in 101-199

Abflug
Departure

CHECK-IN 101-199

ABFLUG
DEPARTURE

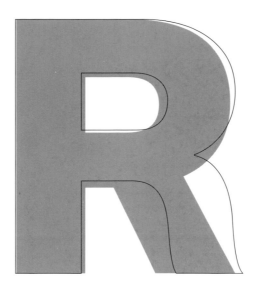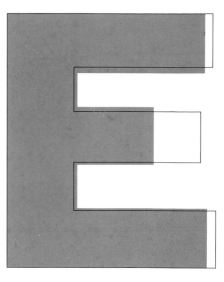

Grey: Interstate Black; Outline black: Helvetica Neue 85 Heavy. The short middle bar of the capital 'E' in Interstate reinforces the legibility of the capital letter.

Akzidenz Grotesk Super

DEPARTURE

Helvetica Neue 85 Heavy

DEPARTURE

Interstate Black

DEPARTURE

Frutiger Next Heavy

DEPARTURE

Franklin Gothic Heavy

DEPARTURE

FF DIN Black

DEPARTURE

Futura T Bold

DEPARTURE

Polo Bold

DEPARTURE

Comparing different fonts helps to finalize the choice of suitable capital letters.

There is just a slight difference between the capitals in these fonts. Apart from the varying widths of the letters, the main distinction lies in the 'R'. The 'E' only looks noticeably different in Interstate.

1.3 Fonts
Choice of Font

Signage system at the Herz-Jesu-Kirche in Völklingen-Ludweiler. The narthex, as the entrance hall of the church, is where you cross into another world. The typography on the heavy steel doors and the light glass wings has a decorative function, and helps the visitor to adapt to the atmosphere of the interior space. The lettering reinforces the transition between the open, profane world outside and the closed, sacred world within, and

Akzidenz-Grotesk provides a highly effective pattern. The straight downstroke of the 'R' combines well graphically with the rigid lines of the other letters. Surprisingly, even the oblique ends of the 'C', 'G' and 'S' have a pleasing effect. They point in no particular direction, and this vagueness is better suited to the typographical pattern than the straight ends of Univers or Helvetica. The text is from Chapter 21 of Revelation.

1
Ebene

→ Aufzug

↘ Ebene 0
0.076 – 0.028

← 1.076 – 1.028

Wayfinding system at the High Performance Computer Centre, Stuttgart University. A rectangular construction hangs down from the ceiling, reflecting a light shining into infinity. The energy of the super-fast computer is conveyed through the glowing information. The letters and figures stand very close to the vertical edges, and Albert-Jan Pool's FF DIN is ideally suited to the slim, orthogonal pillars, as its upright oval and rectangular characters seem to be an integral part of the narrow surface. They also blend in visually with the adjacent perpendicular lines.

Let me make a few personal comments on the queen of sans serif fonts. The publisher Gerd Hatje once told me that Akzidenz Grotesk was Anton Stankowski's favourite font. Its great strength lay in its 'lack of character'. When you look at it closely, the individual letters are not particularly beautiful. The upper case seems too broad in relation to the lower case. This is especially noticeable in the large counter of the capital 'P' and the extensive curves of the 'B'. But when it's all put together on the printed page, the effect is balanced and serene. The efficiency and beauty of the font are most evident in its bold styles: the apertures remain open, and the individual characters become more solid and stable, which is particularly noticeable in the capital 'S'. The greatest merit of this font is probably its formal restraint, which might seem almost crude if the letters are considered one by one. The designer can use it for a whole variety of expressive purposes, by comparison with, say, Otl Aicher's Rotis, which is more restricted. The individual shapes of the latter are in themselves small works of art, but because of their beauty they inevitably take centre stage. Rotis is so dominant that it always looks like Rotis, whereas Akzidenz Grotesk allows for a wide range of applications.

In terms of expression, Akzidenz Grotesk appears quite neutral, but its very imperfection gives it a human touch. It is far more down-to-earth than the timelessly beautiful and serene Helvetica. It is totally unobtrusive and can adapt itself to any situation. In the illustration opposite, Akzidenz Grotesk is used on a crash barrier with two ridges, and yet it is still perfectly legible. This might also be achieved by other fonts, but here the words themselves remain 'undamaged'. It must be said, however, that in comparison with other fonts, it is not all that different from Helvetica and Univers, both of which are outstandingly good and can be used in most projects. If the background were not a crash barrier but an unobtrusive monochrome surface, Univers Condensed would be a better choice. A fine example of this is the wayfinding system at Munich Airport.

The ever handsome but apparently characterless Akzidenz Grotesk was designed by Ferdinand Theinhardt before 1900 and was further developed by Günter Gerhard Lange in 1950.

Wayfinding system at the Pappas Motor Company in Salzburg. The building itself is like a drive-in sculpture. The signage is adapted to the architectural design through a system that accompanies drivers all the way and is drawn from the world of road traffic: the motorist sees the directions in large black lettering on yellow crash barriers, pointing him towards the carwash, the car park, servicing and sales.

The prominent colours help to make the signs instantly readable. The linear structure fits in naturally with the expressiveness of the architectural design and adds an attractive dimension to the leitmotiv of the motor car. The familiar form of the crash barrier helps the visitor to find his way to the correct destination. This simple but robust construction can also withstand the occasional bump. See also page 118.

Of course, Helvetica would also have been suitable for this task, as would Franklin Gothic. The graphic directions here are very prominent, but as the colour and the structure are striking in themselves, the actual form of the lettering needs to preserve a balance and remain discreetly in the background. This is the role to which Akzidenz Grotesk is ideally suited, as its characters are so neutral and unpretentious.

Here we see Akzidenz Grotesk Bold (1) shown above the double ridge of the crash barrier (2). When you look at it from any angle, the height of the letters is shortened by the curved surfaces, as parts of the letters are not vertical. This makes them look squat. In order to make the font look more normal, it was compressed horizontally by a quarter (3), which would not usually be done with any font. When this compressed version is set on the crash barrier (4), the lettering looks back to normal.

1.3 Fonts
Choice of Font

There is little to be gained from comparing Akzidenz Grotesk, Helvetica and Univers with Rotis, which has completely different characteristics and qualities.

The main difference lies in the fact that Rotis displays aesthetic but extremely distinctive forms that can distract the eye. It also comprises a family of fonts, with several branches ranging from serif to sans serif.

PBRPBR

Akzidenz Grotesk Bold, Light

PBRPBR

Neue Helvetica 85 Heavy, 45 Light

PBRPBR

Linotype Univers Basic Bold, Basic Light

PBRPBR

Rotis Semi Sans 75 Extra Bold, 45 Light

Compared with Univers, the Light capital 'P' in Akzidenz Grotesk has a wider counter, making it look slightly out of proportion. In Bold it is much more balanced. The straight downstroke of the capital 'R' in Light seems almost as if it has been tacked on, but in Bold looks much more organic than the curved tail of Helvetica or Univers. The individual characters of Univers are more balanced but also a little dull. In Bold, Akzidenz Grotesk seems the smoothest and the most suitable for trademarks etc. In wayfinding systems, upper case is used for isolated single letters; the best font for these is Univers, whose individual characters in all styles are subtly efficient and effective.

Signage Design

**If in doubt, use
Akzidenz Grotesk.**

The difference between fonts is particularly obvious with the capital 'S'. Akzidenz Grotesk Light looks like a meat hook rather than an organically composed letter, but in Bold this works to its advantage: it is gentle and well balanced, and the curves have aesthetic charm. The Bold Rotis 'S', on the other hand, has very thick ends, which is unsettling. The lower spine of the 'S' in Helvetica is almost oval – a typical feature of this beautiful font. In Univers, the spine of the 'S' is more finely balanced.

Look at the lower-case 'a' in Akzidenz Grotesk Light: the curving base of the stem is too long, and the counter is too broad. This may be why Akzidenz is better suited to longer texts than Helvetica, as these little details hold the letters together like serifs. Interestingly, this stylized form is far less obtrusive in Bold than it is in Helvetica. In Akzidenz Grotesk, the counter is attached directly to the stem, as it is in the American sans serif fonts Trade Gothic and News Gothic. In Helvetica it is more organic, and in Univers it is almost vertical, though still perfectly natural.

Rotis, on the other hand, is a miniature work of art. Otl Aicher, who stressed its functional nature, designed a font that makes an aesthetic statement. Here too the Bold style of Akzidenz Grotesk shows that, of all the fonts, it has the most graphically pleasing counters. The Bold Rotis in particular seems exaggerated. Perhaps this explains why Otl Aicher himself preferred the Light form.

1.3 Fonts
Font Sizes

1.4 Typographical Systems and Type Area
Flexible Grids

The easiest and best way to test the suitability of font sizes in signage is to print them on paper and look at them from the same distance as the observer would.

If the building itself is still at the planning stage, ideally you would find comparable surroundings to test the dimensions of the structures and fonts in an appropriate setting. Concepts that seem good in the office often look too small in practice.

Wayfinding systems must, by definition, be systematic. Font styles and sizes are not chosen arbitrarily, but are graded according to importance. They can be split up, with the largest x-height being a multiple of the smallest, or the sizes can denote a typographical hierarchy (see opposite). In a complex system, all forms may be used and represented in the same size, e.g. on a general display board with an overview of all departments and with a high density of information. In this example, for the information to be contained within a sensible area, the cap height should be between 15 and 25 mm. An observer will stand in front of a main board to look for directions, and so the font can be small because there is a short reading distance and the reader is stationary. This is not the case with directional signs because the target audience is generally on the move and needs to be able to see information from a distance and absorb it quickly without stopping. The cap height should therefore be between 35 and 45 mm if it is to be read from a distance of 2–3 m.

Naturally these sizes depend on the font, and it is essential to test them by first printing them out on paper at full size. Close to a destination, it is possible to indicate several locations on one sign. The visitor might be in a corridor, looking for one particular department, and will not want to jump from one sign to the next to find the right information. The viewing distance can be between 5 and 10 m, and so the font must be correspondingly larger – perhaps between 100 and 150 mm. In developing a system for such information, leading will play an important part. The example opposite is based on a 15 mm unit: the three letter sizes are 15, 45 and 150 mm, corresponding to 1 unit, 3 units and 10 units respectively.

Wayfinding system at the Berufschul-zentrum in Bitterfeld. This grid is flexible: there is no need for a fixed, formally defined arrangement. The grid pattern facilitates flexibility and can be adapted to different architectural settings. The layout is not arbitrary, however: the different sized characters convey a hierarchy.

The x-height of the smallest font is used as a module for the whole grid. The typographical hierarchy relates the three font sizes to the three levels of information. These sizes act like different meshes in a net, enabling the observer to filter out the information he needs. Initially, he simply needs to find his way

within the building, and so the largest size denotes the section of the building and the floor level that he is on. Directions to other areas of the building are in smaller letters, while those to specific parts of the infrastructure are smaller still. The leading of the largest font is a multiple of the smallest.

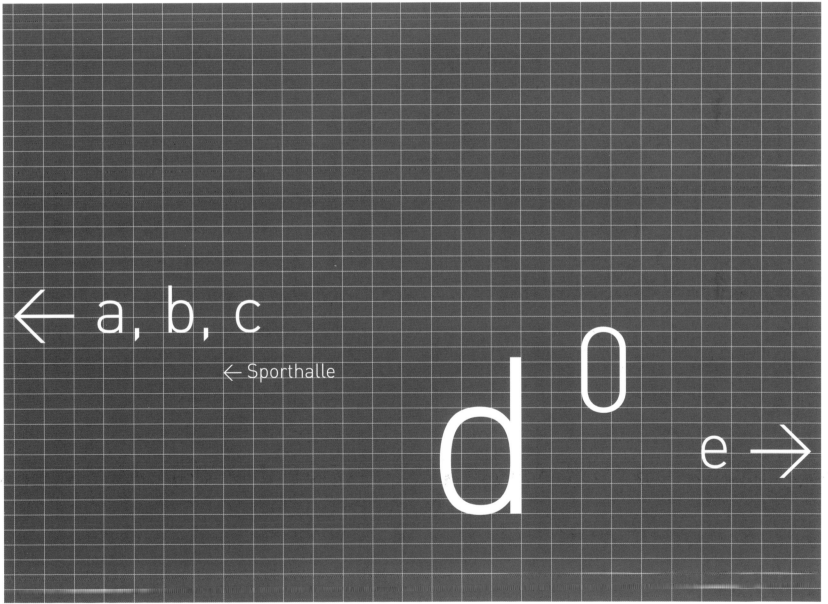

Wayfinding system at Neue Messe, Stuttgart. Design for a typographical grid: here the typographical system determines the formats and the different sizes of the signs.

The typographical grid was developed with the overall aesthetic effect in mind. Each sign consists of four bands of equal height in two different colours. The lettering is still legible against the colourful background because the contrasts between the selected shades are not obtrusive.

To ensure that the bands provide an effective background, the x-height, capital height and descenders must not coincide with the borders between the colours. The bands cut through the letters, so that there are no typographical tails left dangling.

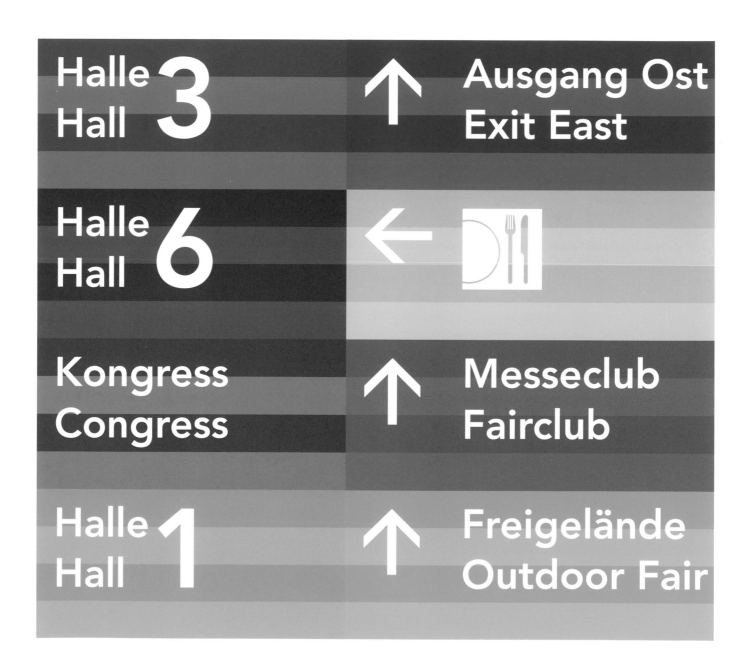

Two straight lines have been drawn through the alphabet in such a way that they do not run too close to the ends of the letters (1). These two lines define a unit, and they can be extended upwards or downwards (2). Three such units define the height of a coloured band.

Laying out two lines of letters according to this principle gives you the line spacing. The distance between the letters and the top of the sign will be correct automatically. The width of the margin between the top and left-hand edges of the sign and the lettering is identical.

1 ABCDEFGHIJKLMNOP
abcdefghijklmnopo

2 Information Toiletten I
Information Toilets Re

43

Signage Design

The sizes of the '6'
and the lettering are
determined by the
sequence of arrows.

**Never ever work
on signage without
a grid!**

In the example below, the square units are determined by the size of the pictogram. The distance between the units is equal to the width of the margin to the left, above and to the right of the lettering. The arrow is smaller than the unit, leaving a large blank space and a clearer separation between direction and information.

In this example, the size of the arrow is calculated by multiplying the smallest font size by 1.75. Arrows should always be placed on the end of the grid. On this type of sign, arrows pointing to the right also belong on the left-hand side.

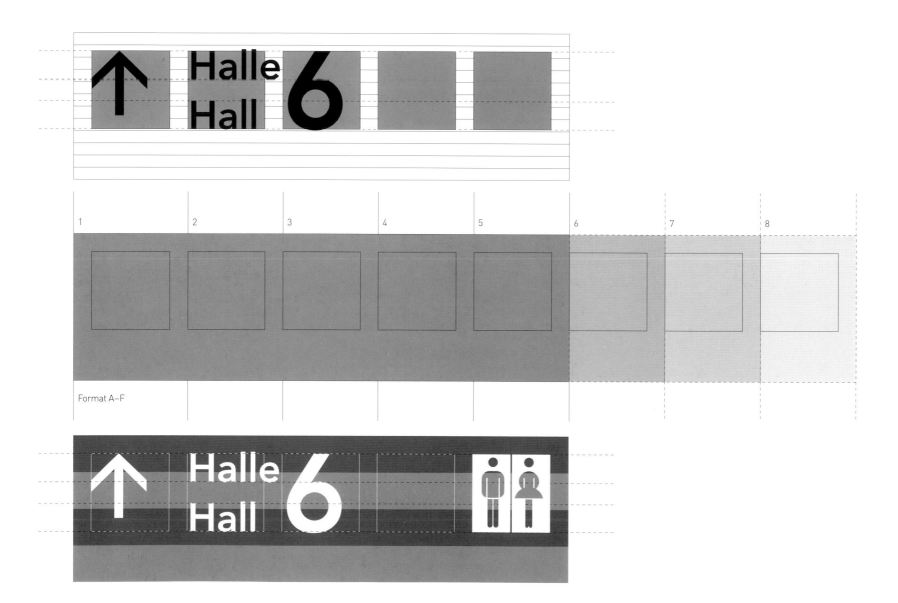

Format A–F

In the examples below, the smallest font size is 200 pt, which gives a sign height of 260 mm (Format F). The slightly larger format (Format E) is based on a factor of 1.75, as is the arrow. The next size up (Format D) is produced by multiplying the height of Format F by 2.417. This factor was based on the assumption that the large-size font in Format F (represented by the '6') should be the same as the small-size font of Format D.

Theoretically, it would be possible to produce a never-ending sign by lining units up next to one another. In reality, the length of signs depends on the content of the information and the character count of the words themselves. Here, the smallest sign is 202 mm wide, and the longest 16,359 mm.

Format A

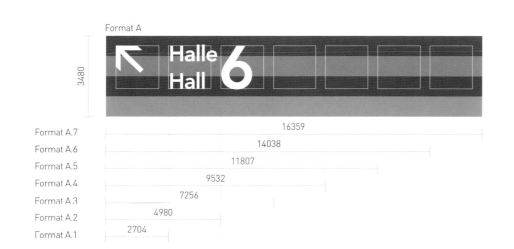

3480

Format A.7	16359
Format A.6	14038
Format A.5	11807
Format A.4	9532
Format A.3	7256
Format A.2	4980
Format A.1	2704

Format B

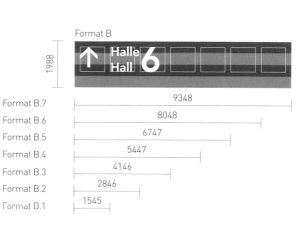

1988

Format B.7	9348
Format B.6	8048
Format B.5	6747
Format B.4	5447
Format B.3	4146
Format B.2	2846
Format B.1	1545

Format C

1260

Format C.7	5916
Format C.6	5093
Format C.5	4270
Format C.4	3447
Format C.3	2624
Format C.2	1801
Format C.1	978

Format D

720

Format D.7	3381
Format D.6	2911
Format D.5	2440
Format D.4	1970
Format D.3	1500
Format D.2	1029
Format D.1	559

Format E

456

Format E.7	2140
Format E.6	1842
Format E.5	1544
Format E.4	1247
Format E.3	949
Format E.2	651
Format E.1	354

Format F

260

Format F.7	1223
Format F.6	1053
Format F.5	883
Format F.4	712
Format F.3	542
Format F.2	372
Format F.1	202

47

Wayfinding system at the trade fair Messe Frankfurt (Stankowski + Duschek). The visual concept is radically functional. There were three guiding principles: the information was stripped down to the basics; it was clear; and the fine balance between reaching those people who want information, but not forcing it on those who don't, was addressed. Each function is given its own distinctive colour: red for directions on ground signs; horizontal green panels for trade fair services; blue squares for parking; yellow for assembling and dismantling services; and grey for technical and internal services. There are three basic forms of information signs:

• general directions on ground signs fixed to the floor
• directions on suspended supports
• signs on supports fixed to the walls

The system functions efficiently using standard and bold Univers, arrows that complement the font, and a few pictograms. The most important information is given in three languages: German in Bold, and English and French in Roman.

The square as a unit. This whole wayfinding system is based on a grid with a minimum unit size of 15 x 15 cm. Theoretically, multiples of this formula could be used to create square formats of different sizes.

In order to limit the variety of forms, only the following dimensions are used:
15 x 15 cm
30 x 30 cm
45 x 45 cm
60 x 60 cm
90 x 90 cm
120 x 120 cm

Adding units: In order to preserve the respective dimensions of particular signs or pylons, modules of the same size are added both horizontally and vertically. Formats should be composed of as few modules as possible.

A margin delimits the type/pictogram area. Here, it is one tenth of the length of the unit, no matter what size of unit is used. For a unit format of 60 x 60 cm, the margin is therefore 6 cm.

If a sign is composed of several units, its margin corresponds to a tenth of its shortest side. For instance, a sign measuring 30 x 90 cm has a margin of 3 cm.

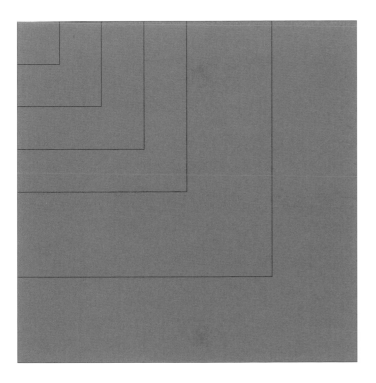

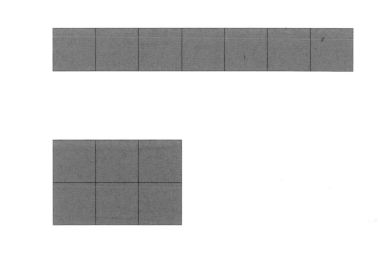

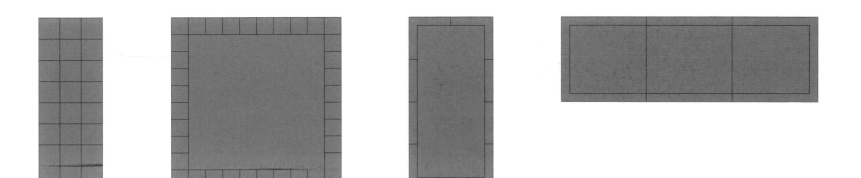

The separate
information panels
in the ground signs
on page 48 – visibly
broken by joints –
adhere to the unit
principle. Each panel
is made up of several
15 x 15 cm units.

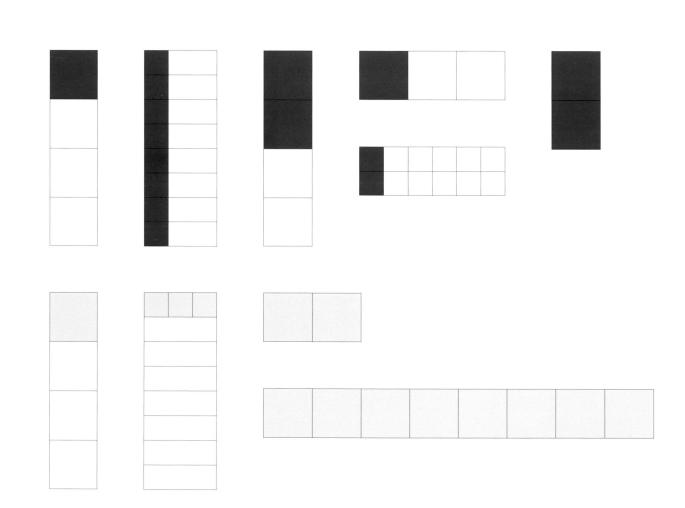

Red squares have been used for directions, both singularly and in vertical strips of multiple units.

Here, green indicates the fair's services. The green units tend to be arranged horizontally. Horizontal coloured bands should be used for restaurant signs, although length will depend on the architectural context.

The secondary colours are blue, yellow and grey, which only occur as individual squares (i.e. no additional coloured units may be added).

In general, when colours have been used in this way for identification, they should only be combined with the basic white background. In other words, information for different areas should be placed on separate signs. In a few cases, information from other areas – if possible, with pictograms – can be incorporated.

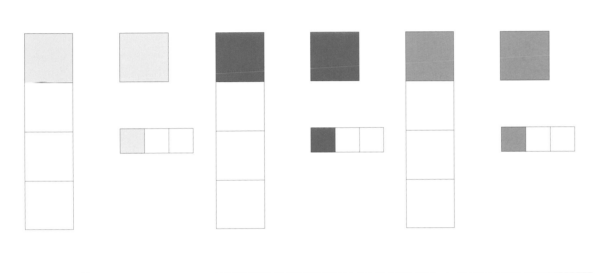

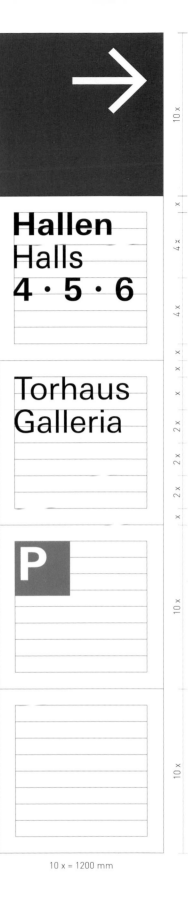

10 x = 1200 mm

1.4 Typographical Systems and Type Area
Format-dependent Grids

There are many different ways of designing signage formats. Mathematical series such as DIN standards and Fibonacci numbers may be helpful, but working exclusively with squares or rectangles can also be effective, the length of which can be adapted to the specific requirements. The examples on this page have been created for an airport (arrow, pictogram, single words).

Wayfinding system at Stuttgart Airport. The horizontal and vertical sides of each sign follow a ratio of 6:5. The size and impact of the signs work well: the large surface can be seen from a considerable distance, highlighting the fact that it contains important information. This would not have been possible with a narrow format. In order to maximize on visual impact, the format is available in three sizes that have been developed in response to specific requirements. The grey sign can be split up into eight bands for different airlines or to guide motorists through car parks.

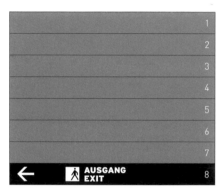

↑	→	←	↑	→	↑	→

ABFLUG 1, 2, 3, 4
DEPARTURE 1, 2, 3, 4

CHECK-IN 101–103
CHECK-IN 201–210
CHECK-IN 301–338
CHECK-IN 401–410

ANKUNFT 3, 4, 5
ARRIVAL 3, 4, 5

TOILETTEN
TOILETS

BESUCHERTERRASSE
VISITORS TERRACE

REISEMARKT
TRAVEL POINT

RUNDFLÜGE
SIGHTSEEING FLIGHTS

KONFERENZZENTRUM
KONFERENCE CENTRE

FUNDBÜRO
LOST AND FOUND

SCHLIESSFÄCHER
LOCKERS

AUSGANG
EXIT

INFORMATION

TREFFPUNKT 3, 5
MEETING POINT 3, 5

S-BAHN
SUBWAY

SHOPS

RESTAURANT

APOTHEKE
PHARMACY

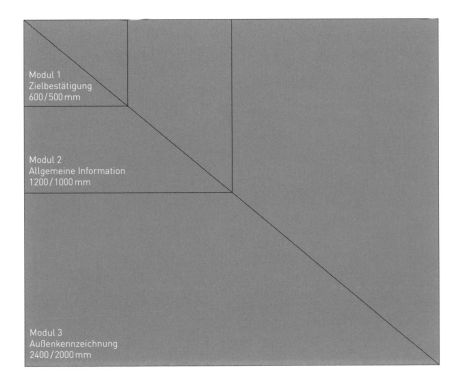

Modul 1
Zielbestätigung
600 / 500 mm

Modul 2
Allgemeine Information
1200 / 1000 mm

Modul 3
Außenkennzeichnung
2400 / 2000 mm

Left: Diagram showing the three different sizes of sign in the wayfinding system at Stuttgart Airport.

For the Munich Olympic Games in 1972, Otl Aicher and Gerhard Joksch designed a system of pictograms that is still in use today. Visually, it has retained a sleek, modern look with its clear, faultless representation of forms and figures. Notice, for instance, how the smoke curls up from the cigarette, swirling from between the ash and the stem and not, as in so many poor imitations, above the ash itself. In order to avoid the licence fee for using this masterpiece of pictogram design, which has been extended to over 1,000 forms by ERCO, imitators have plagiarized and cheapened it. A clear example of this can be seen in the top right corner of this page. The figure in the grey square leaning backwards in the wheelchair is a sad reflection of the self-confident, upright man in the original (opposite). Another oversight lies in the shape of the hands, which point upwards instead of downwards. In a natural position, the hands would rest on the arms of the wheelchair.

It is possible to order a CD-ROM from ERCO which contains all the pictograms and can be used for layout purposes. However, if the pictograms themselves are used, the company or architect must obtain a licence and include an acknowledgment.

As Otl Aicher's pictogram series is based on a grid, his signs take on a high degree of abstraction. It is by no means an exaggeration to say that his handling of the subject-matter set the benchmark for pictogram design. Don't let this put you off devising your own series, however. Pictogram design can be really fun! New pictograms have to be different – not just slightly different, as we see all too often in the world around us. Sarah Rosenbaum's attractive scribbled drawings for the 1994 Olympic Games in Lillehammer look like cave paintings. Another alternative approach, this time by intégral ruedi baur, can be found on page 171.

353

098

004

Opposite, top left: Pictograms for the Mexico Olympics in 1968, under the direction of Lance Wyman – in keeping with the era and the country.

Opposite, top centre: Masaru Katzumie's pictograms for the Tokyo Olympics of 1964. Next to the cheerful and colourful signs for the Mexico Games, these clearly set out to develop a graphic, abstract system with a high degree of symbolism.

Opposite, top right: This clearly takes the ERCO pictogram of the disabled man as its model, but this one falls far short of the original.

Masaru Katzumie's series of pictograms paved the way for Otl Aicher. He further developed the style by standardizing the figures, which are represented by head, trunk, arms and legs. Movement is depicted through diagonals. The consistency of the structural syntax is especially clear with the different sports, though obviously it is not so marked in other areas of the system.

We shall confine ourselves here to a single system, which graphically is the most sophisticated and refined of them all. However, from page 128 onwards, in the third chapter of this book, you will find a large number of pictograms designed by different companies for particular projects.

However, from page 128 onwards, in the third chapter of this book, you will find a large number of pictograms designed by different companies for particular projects.

All rules are doctrinaire, and especially this one: Otl Aicher's pictograms are the best and should be used!

076

Otl Aicher's disabled man sits upright. This is not only an accurate observation, but also endows the figure with dignity. He is clearly sitting well above the axis of the wheel, which is also structurally correct. In the grey pictogram opposite (top left), the wheel ends in the middle of his back.

612

195

019

361

356

ERCO/Otl Aicher
353 Fur goods
098 Stairs up
004 Ladies' toilets
076 Disabled
612 Football
195 Restaurant
019 No smoking
361 Sex shop
356 Toys

55

There are two basic types of arrow: in the top left arrow (1), opposite, the terminals of the arrowhead are parallel to the shaft, whereas in the red arrow below it (2), the terminals are cut off at right angles. The terminals of the first example seem aggressively sharp and tend to lack clarity from a distance. The second example is geometrically more distinct, but it contains four different angles: the slant of the arrowhead (45^0), the shaft (0^0), the base of the shaft (90^0) and the terminals of the head (135^0). The first arrow only has three angles (0^0, 45^0 and 90^0). This may seem just a minor detail, but it makes the first arrow more cohesive and precise.

The first arrow, or variations of this type, is used throughout the UK, particularly on road signs where it is often seen without a shaft. German road signs, in contrast, tend to feature the second type of arrow, with terminals at a right angle. The grey arrow above, where shaft and head are separated, is used by the German railways. This design may be based on the idea that the joining point where the shaft and head meet often seems optically thicker and is potentially confusing, but the separation makes this arrow look ugly. In the arrows opposite, the shaft is inserted into the head, and there is no adverse thickening effect.

Arrow 1 is in FF DIN Light, while arrow 2 is in Thesis The Sans Extra Light Expert. The proportions of the two arrows are similar (Thesis grey, FF DIN black), although the barbs are more tapered in Thesis.

There are whole books on the subject of arrows, and of course the examples shown here aren't the only varieties. Just as with fonts, there is a wide choice available, but here we shall deal with just two types that are suitable for wayfinding systems. The arrows on page 168 should give you some insight into just what can be done.

1

2

Wayfinding system at the HypoVereinsbank in Luxembourg. The arrow is a universal symbol. Arrows can be thick or thin, heavy or light. Blunt arrows lack grace, but if they are too sharp, they become indistinct. This system used three arrows in three Frutiger styles, which created the optimal balance between the letters and arrows.

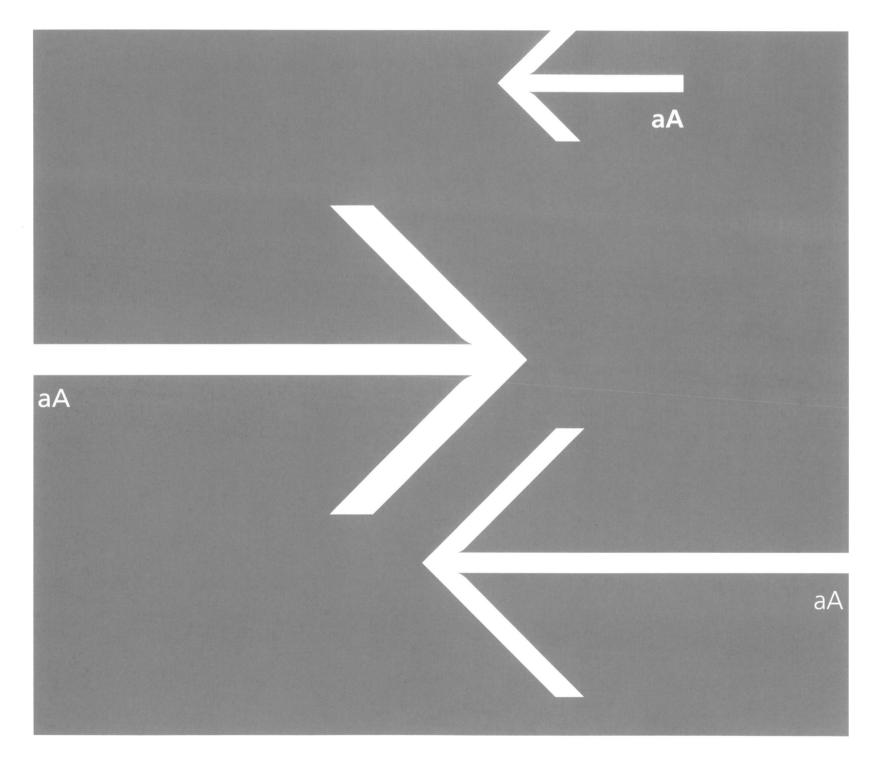

Wayfinding system at the HypoVereinsbank in Luxembourg. The arrows have an essential function – to direct road traffic – but they can also be used as a feature of the design. In this underground car park, the large arrows create a decorative white pattern to relieve the gloom. See also pages 79 and 105.

Interestingly, human beings do not have the ability to register colours. You can test this for yourself by choosing, say, a shade of red from a colour chart and then trying to commit it to memory. Put the chart on one side, and then a few seconds later open it up again at the different shades of red. You will have great difficulty identifying which one you chose. We tend to distinguish colours only in broad categories: blue, red, yellow, green etc. Even the borderlines between these can be questionable, and of course colours also change according to the light.

Wayfinding systems that are based purely on colour coding can therefore only be of limited efficiency, as the system first has to be learned. The learning element can be facilitated by the use of forms – a blue flower, for instance, or a green elephant. This is greatly simplified if there is not much information to be conveyed.

Hülshoff

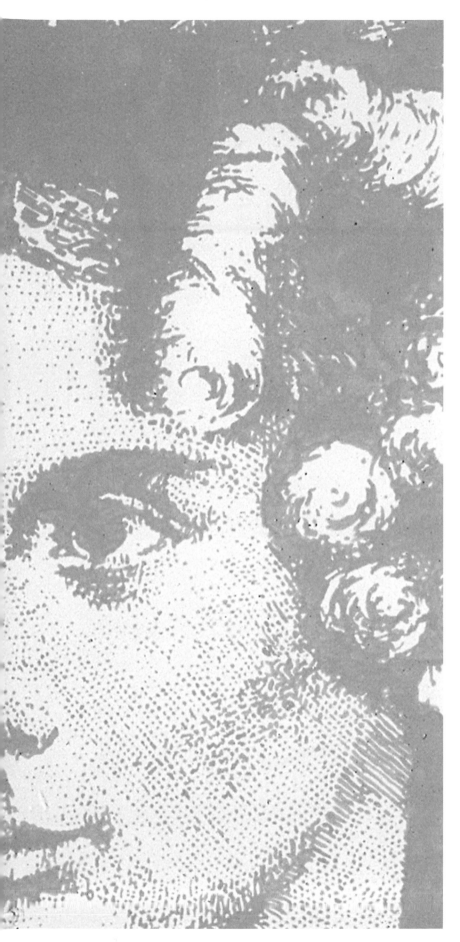

Wayfinding system at the Bollwerk Service Centre, Landesbank Baden-Württemberg, Stuttgart. In the bank's underground car park, the six different levels are denoted by six pictures and six colours. The pictures are of historical German figures whose images have appeared on banknotes.

Each level is given a familiar motif that does not require any special knowledge. This method also makes the car park seem friendlier. Short biographies on the walls brighten up what would otherwise be a somewhat cheerless atmosphere. See also page 94.

Colour alone does not help in wayfinding. If it is combined with a form, the result will be an attention-grabbing image that can be used to codify a section or level of the building.

1.7 Colour

Wayfinding system at the Neue Messe, Stuttgart, based on dual colouring. The architects reacted to this strong emphasis on colour by leaving the buildings themselves in the natural, dull colours of their materials.

The steel had to be painted in order to protect it against corrosion, but it was given a neutral grey coat that did not compete with the bright colours of the wayfinding system. See also pages 88–89 and 102.

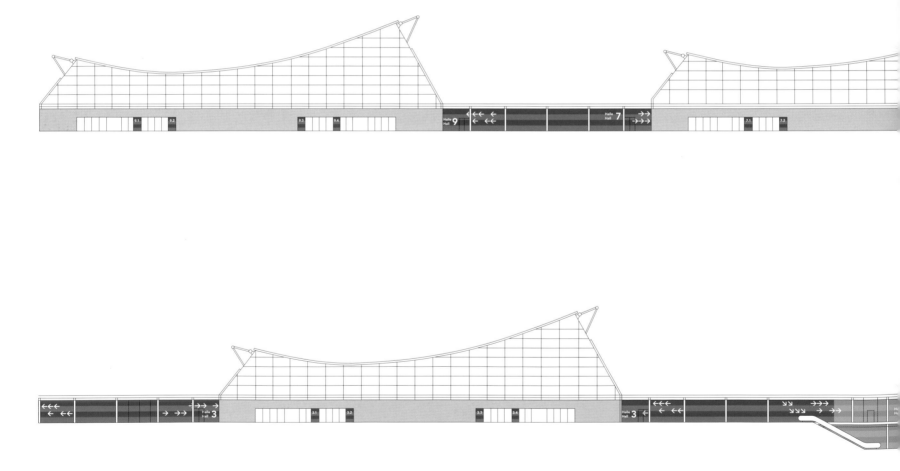

The system uses various formats that sometimes conflict with the geometry of the architecture. In the signs for the exhibition halls, for example, the grid of the façade has dictated the format of the sign. On exposed concrete walls, signs would be too small and inconspicuous, and so instead of using the format system, the information is placed on the architecture itself. This means that the format is provided by the architectural context, and the typographical system has to be developed in accordance with the surfaces and materials provided. Translucent transfer tape is used on glass, and colours, arrows and letters are painted on walls. See also pages 42–47.

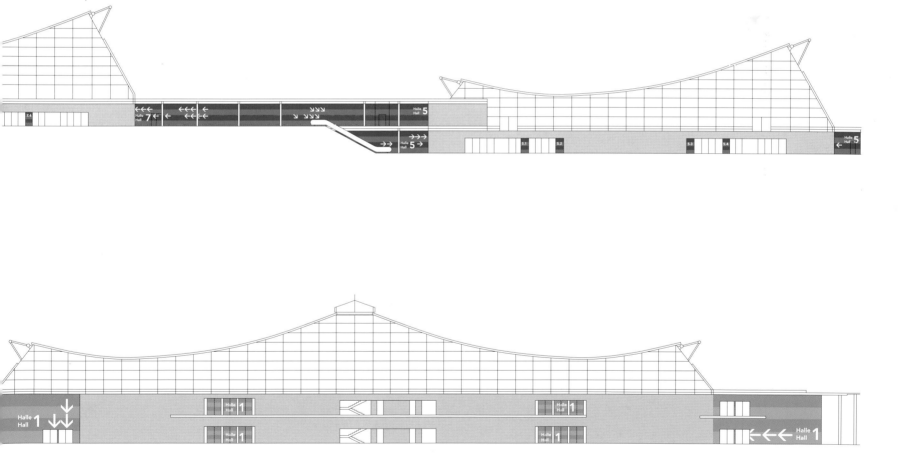

1.7 Colour
Colour Language

Otl Aicher describes how he travelled across country on a motorbike and found himself in a country inn. The violet of the table napkin inspired the reddish blue for Munich Airport. The management rejected it, however, and Aicher withdrew from the project, which was completed by Eberhard Stauss.

In complex wayfinding systems, colour can help to arrange the information hierarchically. The example opposite shows how it can be structured for airline passengers and the difference colour coding can make. In the bottom row, the red notices are for passenger information, infrastructure is white on black, and retail is black on white. Red is the most eye-catching colour and therefore communicates the most important information, allowing someone who is in a hurry to ignore other notices. This three-colour system can cater for different requirements. If it used just one or two colours, it would not be able to structure the information so efficiently and would still require the same number of signs.

Colours have certain cultural and historical associations, although these can differ vastly in different countries around the world. Red, white and black, for instance, might be seen as fascist, and the old Reich flag was in precisely these colours. Purple is often associated with cardinals, though bishops now wear violet and cardinals scarlet, in commemoration of the blood of the martyrs. Gold and silver symbolize power. Black is the colour of mourning, and red and white are also connected with Socialism. It is time that we emancipated ourselves from these associations and regarded colours as values in themselves.

In airport wayfinding systems, you will often see black lettering on a yellow background. This is because yellow is known to attract attention, and black lettering on luminous yellow is easy to read. If all the airport signs in the world were designed in the same way, passengers would certainly find their way around much more readily, and indeed this idea has been considered. But would it really be a good thing? In the United States, emergency exit signs are usually white with the word 'EXIT' in red or green, whereas in Europe they are green with white lettering or pictograms. Would it make sense for them to be standardized? In Germany, motorway signs are blue and ordinary road signs are yellow, while in Switzerland and Italy the former are green and the latter are blue. So which colour should be used for which purpose? There are practically no colours left for standardization, and in any case uniformity would surely mean cultural impoverishment. Munich Airport rejoices in a lovely reddish blue, which is original and quite different from all the colours of the architecture around it. This shade is striking and functional but by no means intrusive. The yellow of the illuminated signs, by contrast, seems harsh, and although it is efficient, it has a disturbingly aggressive effect. At times even the right colour can be wrong.

Wayfinding system at Stuttgart Airport. There is a striking contrast between the text and the background in all three signage areas (passenger information, infrastructure and retail). The combination of blue and white for traffic is a commonly recognized signage coding and has been retained here for the car parks.

In both Germany and the UK, green is the colour used for emergency exits and is therefore of limited use in wayfinding systems. The yellow background matches the Lufthansa logo.

Colour coding is practical for airport signs. The division into passenger information, infrastructure and retail is helpful for passengers in a hurry, who need only concentrate their attention on, for instance, the red signs. They can take in additional information, but they can also shut it out.

Colour coding facilitates wayfinding. The examples below show that the division into three areas of reference does not necessarily entail more signs.

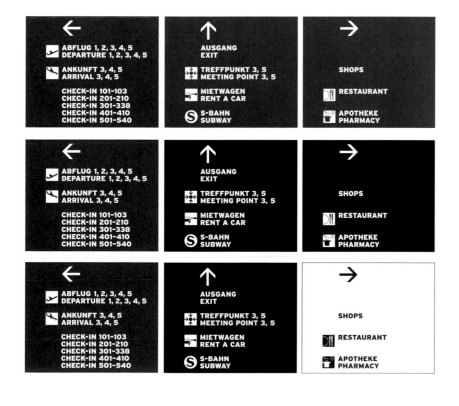

1.7 Colour
Colour Contrast

Wayfinding system at the Elektrotechnische Institute II, Stuttgart University. Silver-painted bands on the wall contain directions to the institutes and departments in dark green and purple.
If the lettering had had a white background, it would have looked garish and the effect of the colours would have been greatly reduced. These dark shades go well together with the silver base and form a discreet unit.

The silver bands blend in with the grey of the concrete walls, creating an almost sculptured effect, which makes the system look like it is formally integrated into the architecture.

Black lettering is often used on bright-coloured backgrounds. This may work, but it is not particularly attractive. The black radiates out into the surrounding colour zone and merges with the background colour. White letters on a bright background stand out more clearly – even against yellow, provided the shade is dark enough.

Coloured lettering can be quite decorative, but it can make a very strong impact and needs to be used sparingly. Coloured letters can also convey a message – for instance, they may indicate that you are on a particular floor. In order to do this efficiently, they must be set in dull surroundings as otherwise the different elements may find themselves in competition with one another. Generally, coloured lettering is problematic and less expressive than white or black.

In wayfinding systems, contrast is important for ease of reading. If coloured lettering is used on a bright background, the contrast is weak. The optimal contrast is white against dark colours and black against bright colours.

Against a coloured background white lettering always looks best, but only if there is sufficient contrast. Even with bright colours, or against dark shades of yellow, white is most effective. Black lettering tends to merge with the background and make the colour look dirty.

Wayfinding system at the Neue Messe, Stuttgart. Directions to areas of the infrastructure are coded in yellow. In order to create a proper contrast, different combinations of yellow are printed in silkscreen.

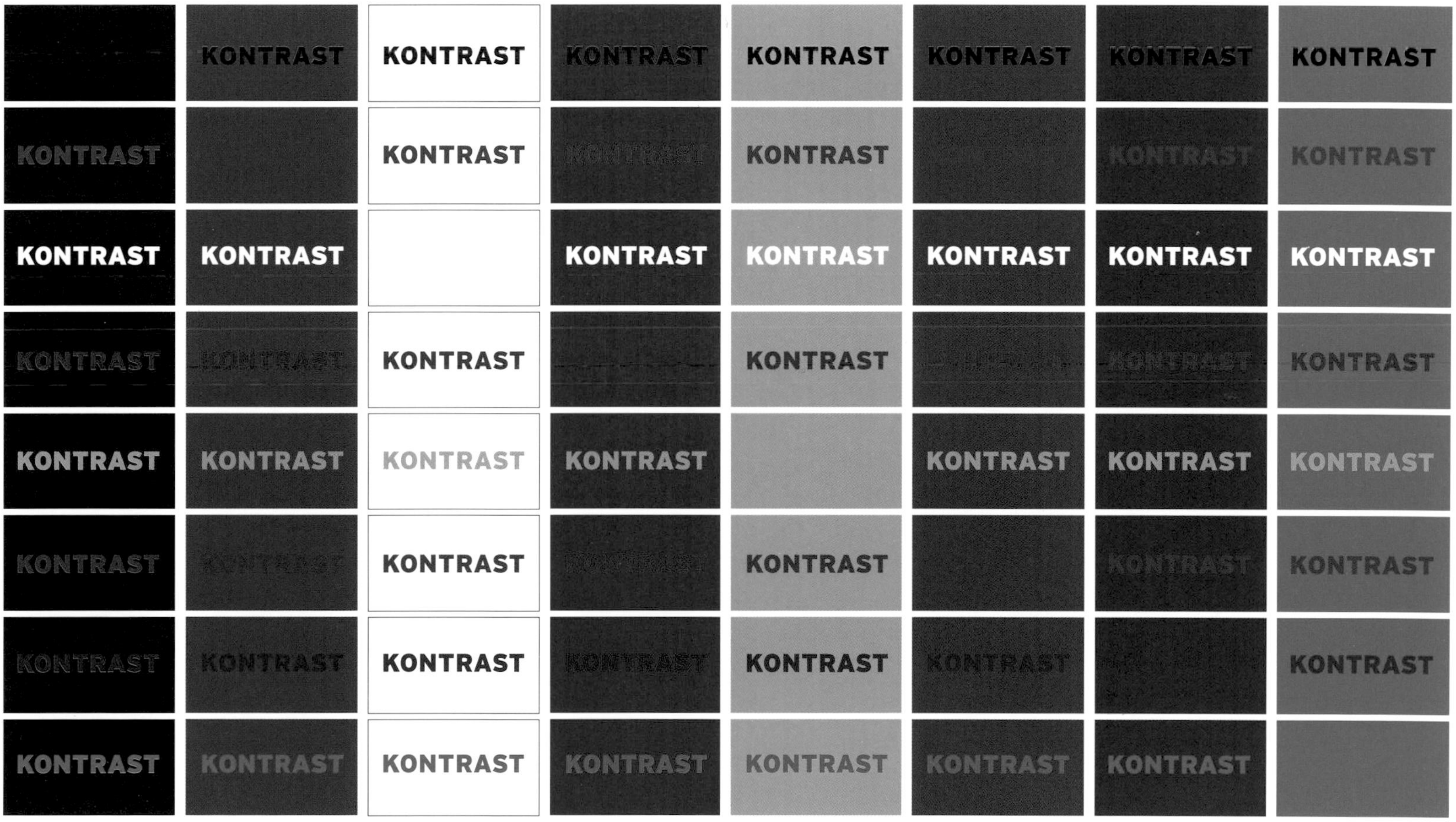

Garderobe Wardrobe

Imbiss Snack

1.7 Colour
Colour Systems

There are various colour systems on the market, including Pantone, NCS (Natural Colour System), HKS (an abbreviation of three German colour manufacturers, Hostmann-Steinberg Druckfarben, Kast + Ehinger Druckfarben and H. Schmincke & Co.) and RAL (Reichsausschuss für Lieferbedingungen). However, not every company that develops such systems also produces the colours.

All colour systems have been devised by individuals or teams; they are not mathematical formulae but designs. There are systems in which the range of colours has been systematically grouped from one extreme to the other (e.g. Brillux, NCS), although they do not contain every possible shade because many are so similar that our eyes can't tell the difference. When infinitesimally graduated shades are placed in sequence, it is impossible for the naked eye to distinguish between them. NCS is the Scandinavian equivalent of the German RAL. It is logically and comprehensibly constructed rather

like a globe: the poles are black and white, and the four directions are blue, red, green and yellow. In the crescent-shaped discs that you could cut out of the sphere, the intermediate shades are in the middle. RAL was formed in 1925 as a joint initiative by private commerce and the then government of the Democratic Weimar Republic. Its original task was to unify and standardize technical supplies with a view to rationalization. No other colour system offers so many subtly differentiated shades of grey. The RAL chart RAL-K-5 contains shades unlike any others. The colours are easily available everywhere as paint, but unfortunately are not available for offset printing. Under the name of RAL-Design, RAL also offers a colour chart with an extended range.

The Pantone colour chart (PMS, or Pantone Matching System) is a widely used system in the printing industry. The choice of dark and grey-scale shades is, however, a little narrow.

Signage system at
Viavai Winebar. The
use of transfer tape
has created a subtle
contrast and makes
the glass look
sandblasted; in the
evening, it reflects the
light and is luminous.

The selection of
colour systems and
manufacturers below
is purely subjective.
There are many
such systems on the
market, and a good
designer should take
the trouble to find
the right colours
and manufacturer for
himself. Any planner
should welcome
variety, and must
expect to work with
a lot of different
systems.

There are many manufacturers of transfer tape on the market. In choosing one, you need to make sure that the company can supply all the necessary elements of the system – i.e. a package of ink, printing materials and laminates. You can cut out letters or large areas with a plotter, but without this technology many projects would be unthinkable. Transfer tape can be either cast or extruded. A cast film is better quality and, depending on the manufacturer and the finish, has a longer lifespan of between 5 and 10 years (i.e. it doesn't shrink, the colours remain fast, it is UV-resistant, it doesn't fade, is weatherproof, and does not break or become brittle). It is also possible to have your own colours incorporated in the manufacturing process of the film.

Brillux is a new colour system designed by Rahe & Rahe and is a complex programme with finely graduated shades for varnishes and emulsions. Unfortunately, these colours are not available for printing either.

HKS is a standardized colour system for printing. The range is quite restricted, but it boasts beautiful colours.

Marabu offers a colour range for screenprinting, with many interesting variations.

The Swiss manufacturer Printcolor produces excellent quality colours and also offers first-class and reliable advice.

Le Corbusier designed a colour chart for the firm Salubra, and the individual shades can be successfully mixed and matched. This is an unconventional range, available for painting walls.

The Sikkens system is similar – the colours are available for varnishes and emulsions, and they offer a wide range of subtly graduated shades.

A deep vertical black. Light disappears and the eye finds no focal point, but simply wanders around aimlessly and endlessly. The space between the black wall and the observer expands. The black surface tilts and the light falls at an angle and, as if under a microscope, reveals a structure, the surface of which forms a crude web like fine grains of sand. It is made of light and shadow, and the mixture of bright hills and dark valleys creates a new tone of dark grey. The next tone is a lake. It stretches out horizontally, and moonlight shines on its silken surface. The colour liquifies and begins to shimmer as the darkness brightens and the depths take on a silver sheen.

A wayfinding system is an intervention into an existing work. The architect retains the copyright for this work, and any changes, including graphic additions, require his permission. The graphic elements will therefore normally be planned after the architectural and design parameters have already been laid down. It is a rare privilege if architecture and graphic design can be developed in unison at an early stage. And even then, the architect's ideas will determine the world of colours, materials and surfaces far more than any input from the designer. Naturally, there will always be the odd exception to this generalization, when an architect responds to the graphic design.

The designer has to ask himself the following questions: Is there an existing colour harmony from which new tones can be developed? Or do the materials clash? In a dull space, is it better to install graphics with restrained colours, or would a colourful focus be more attractive? Anything is possible, but not everything works. The colour of the graphics can dominate sections of a building to their advantage or disadvantage. Sometimes a loud colour will work, but other times it won't, and dull shades can be discreetly effective or disappear altogether.

Design for an exhibition at the Roman Baths, Baden-Baden. The remains of the baths lie trapped between an electricity substation and a low-roofed underground car park. The roof is oppressive, and if it were white, the ribbed ceiling would impose itself too much on the foreground. The architects Kränzle + Fischer-Wasels therefore had it painted in anthracite, so that it looks rather like a night sky.

According to one old wives' tale, painting small spaces in bright colours makes them look bigger. This isn't true. In order to look at an object, you must direct your eye to it and create a line of sight; light is then reflected from that object back to your pupil. This is how we perceive the physical presence of, say, a wall and can determine its distance with a fairly precise degree of accuracy. The area is thus defined in terms of a limited surface. The rays of light are like messengers. If there is no longer any reflection to send back the light, there will be no precise information about the physical presence of the wall or about where it comes to an end. Thus the space will seem bigger, because the walls that delimit the room cannot be discerned and the boundaries become indistinct. Small spaces can therefore be made to look bigger if they are painted in dark colours.

1.7 Colour
Grey

Far left: Colour of
the walls, Sikkens
ON.0069.

Left: Colour of
the ceilings,
NCS S 0502-B.

Grey is duller than white. When a colour design was proposed for the renovation of the main E.ON administration building in Munich, white was chosen for the walls and ceilings. Our suggestion, however, was to paint them grey. This was a reaction to the irregular structure of the old building, with its many projections and recesses, and the various additions of different-coloured high-grade steel and aluminium, the suspended ceilings of expanded metal etc. It seemed better to us to calm things down with a colour that would act as a protective skin. The offices, therefore, were not given stark, white walls but a warm coat of grey.

If you were to compare grey and white side by side, there is a danger that you would dismiss the former for being too dark. However, if you try it out in a room, you will find that without the direct comparison with white it no longer seems as dark. It is always advisable to work with a full-scale model under real conditions in order to form a balanced judgment. However, before going ahead with such a model, you should first get a lighting engineer to test whether the colour you are planning to use will conform to the prescribed minimal light values.

Another useful tip is to try out a few different shades, both for your own benefit, to see if you have made the right choice, and for the client, so that he can judge the effect for himself. All colours apart from white absorb light, but does this mean that we should paint every room white? Of course it doesn't. However, it is important to work out precisely which walls are the most important reflectors. They are not – or are very rarely – the exterior walls that contain the windows, which can be painted in colour. In modern offices, partition walls are often made of wood, or the division between workspaces is provided by built-in office furniture. What is left is the ceiling, together with a few passageways. Here the colours can be strong without having too much effect on the lighting.

A grey wall can be less grey than a white wall because white gets dirty. Also the surrounding colours are reflected in the white. This can be an intentional form of decoration – when, for instance, a blue wall throws a bluish shadow onto the white surface.

Wayfinding system at the main E.ON administration building in Munich. Grey walls and ceilings form a restrained background for the colours of the glass partition walls, which bear transparent coloured silkscreen bands on transparent film. See also pages 90–91 and 288–93.

1.7 Colour
White

Signage system at Viavai Winebar, Stuttgart. White lettering in relief gives the place a friendly feel and encourages sociability. The inscription reads: Making new mistakes.

White on white provides an interesting combination. Its charm lies in its minimal contrast. If the background is matt, the letters can be glossy or in relief. It would be interesting to experiment with a wayfinding system that dispensed with colour and only worked with contrasting surfaces, e.g. glossy black on matt black.

Wayfinding system at the state insurance building (Landesversicherungsanstalt) in Augsburg. Large, glossy white numbers and signs on a matt white wall indicate the code numbers of different insurances. The lettering here has a decorative function, though this could just as well be a means of conveying information, providing a pleasant way of introducing various facets of the company. See also pages 78 and 113.

1.7 Colour
Silver

Wayfinding system at the medical centre of Alsterdorf Evangelical Foundation. Silver lettering on a white background is more problematic than vice versa, as the white surface reflects a great deal of light and can flood the thin silver text. The issue was identified, tested and discussed with the client before the work was carried out.

White and silver are not colourful, and in combination are light and incorporeal. Silver reflects the colours of its surroundings and fits in easily with anything. The contrast between white and silver, however, can cause major problems. Depending on the light, silver lettering on a white background can be very difficult to read, and it is essential to warn the client about this danger. During the design phase and before any final commitment, it's a good idea to make models in the chosen colours and materials, and discuss them with the architect, the client and potential users. The main problem with silver lettering on a white background is that you can't see anything from some angles. From certain standpoints, the silver looks white; if you then move slightly, the writing may look almost like black on white. This may seem immaterial, as you are likely to be on the move anyway, and the overall effect often makes it worthwhile.

This wayfinding system uses squares as its basic form. Information is given on white surfaces, and directions on silver. In outside areas, the signs are on white and silver film. Inside they consist of three-dimensional plaques, which have been placed in rhythmic sequences to create an animated surface, like that of a lake rippled in the breeze. The optical movement relieves the rigidity of the square format. See also pages 122 and 124–125.

The staircases in the medical centre have been painted silver, and the pattern of white bands gets thinner from from top to bottom.

Wayfinding system at the state insurance building in Augsburg. The dark silver (RAL 9023 pearl dark grey) provides an excellent contrast to the white lettering. From certain angles, the silver looks black.

Wayfinding system at Kronen Carré, Stuttgart. The silver tone is set by the material: high-grade steel with glass beads on a sandstone base, silver-bronze paint on the plastered walls, and silver film on the glass surfaces. Silver reflects other colours around it, and the interplay between lettering and colours creates a pleasant harmony within the integrated design of text and architecture.

Silver paint is particularly difficult to apply, as it does not appear even and shows up the strokes of the brush or roller. There are paints available that can overcome this problem, but they are very expensive. Again it is advisable to make samples initially to see if there are any undesired effects before final commitment. See also page 101.

Wayfinding system at HypoVereinsbank in Luxembourg. The silver room numbers are silkscreen printed directly onto the exposed concrete walls. Earlier, the same concrete mix was used in several DIN-A4 samples with different shades of silver to work out the most suitable colour.

The architect and client were then shown the samples on the spot. The shade that was chosen contrasted best with the grey of the concrete and was the least dazzling.

1.7 Colour
Red

Wayfinding system at the Fachhochschule, Osnabrück. The floor levels are in RAL 3018 (strawberry red). The handful of red words form a stark contrast to the black text and white ceiling. This approach is designed to emphasize these particular items of information. A fairly moderate shade has been chosen, so that the red doesn't seem too garish against the black. See also pages 202–7.

RAL 3018 strawberry red: The name of this paint brings summer to mind. The hot, overbearing midday sun takes the sharpness away from this shade of red, as the heat of the day turns our actions to slow motion. It is the bluish shadow of a summer cloud that passes over the rash red flame and dulls its fire. The red remains red – still powerful but no longer aggressive.

There's no such thing as plain red. Red painted on a steel pipe will be strong, but on wood it becomes duller. It's a powerful colour, and that can create problems. When it's chosen, it should be seen as an opportunity to make a statement (see pages 222–25, wayfinding system at Stuttgart University's cafeteria). If you want red, make it a real red – fluorescent, or strawberry. All colours have many different shades. The so-called primary colours – red, yellow, green and blue – are really metaphors. When we mention them, we see them in block form, as in children's building bricks, but in an architectural context they are generally too loud and dominant.

Signage Design

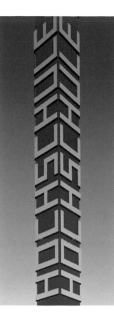

Signage system at the Hochschule der Medien, Stuttgart. This media college consists of one old and one new building, and an extension is now at the planning stage. The authorities wanted one of the buildings to display the school's identity. Our proposal, however, was to separate the name from the buildings themselves, and to draw all three of them together visually in a pole sign.

Red is the college's basic colour, and the red streak in the green environment sends out a strong signal. The inscription is in relief, and to make it easier to read, it has been painted in the complementary colour green.

Wayfinding system at the cafeteria in Stuttgart University. Red is a primary colour, and like yellow and blue it is 'loud' in an architectural context. These colours have the same effect as strong geometrical forms – circles, triangles, squares – and tend to be self-centred in the sense that they do not fit in easily with their surroundings. But despite their dominant nature, sometimes this feature can be deliberately exploited as part of the design. In this illustration, the striking glow of the red is an effective means of visually separating the information structure from that of the architecture. The latter is in the form of a spatial grid, and so the alienating effect of the colour helps to ensure that the vertical lines of information do not merge into the upright architectural supports. See also pages 222–25.

1.7 Colour
Yellow

In some German airports, Lufthansa has its own signs (third sign on the right). In this illustration the Lufthansa sign competes with the airport information signs, which are in a lighter shade of yellow. This is another argument against the use of yellow, particularly in German airports.

Sunflower yellow, saffron yellow, gorse yellow...there are many different shades of yellow, and people associate them with many different things. Corn seeds take you back to nature, lemon yellow is seductive, lime yellow is more bitter, traffic-light yellow puts you on your guard, sunlight yellow brings joy to the heart, and honey yellow is sweet. Yellow goes well with red or green.

In many German airports, yellow is the background colour for signage. This is probably because yellow is particularly suited to sending out signals, but in the context this actually counts against it. The aggressive tone disturbs the architectural harmony. The airport environment is unsettling, with people rushing to and fro and loud announcements constantly breaking into conversations. Many products in everyday use carry warning signs in yellow. Amber traffic lights warn you that you have to stop or go. A yellow glow penetrates like the sun: it makes you feel like you need to protect yourself. Household articles such as pots and pans, telephones and ashtrays are rarely yellow; they tend to be in more muted colours.

Wayfinding system at Stuttgart Airport. For this project, the authorities wanted to use yellow for primary information. This is standard for German airports and therefore makes sense. Our argument, however, was based on architectural and psychological factors.

Yellow is an aggressive colour and is seen as an intrusive element in the architectural context. To test it out, signs were mounted in red (see page 17) and yellow. In the silver-grey environment of the airport, the red signs worked better.

1.7 Colour
Yellow

Information and wayfinding system for cultural and historic buildings in Dresden. In such a large city, visitors need to find their way efficiently, without any hitches. A coding system was designed to be as attractive as possible, and was based on the distance between the onlooker and his destination – the further away he or she was, the more abstract the information. As the visitor nears the destination, the information becomes more detailed.

The soft yellow (NCS S 0540-Y) on the posts responds to the brightness of the sandstone. The sensitive use of colour attracts attention without imposing on the urban landscape. This special Dresden yellow, which is also a reference to the city's heraldry, is supported by a silver-grey base (RAL 7048 pearl mouse grey); the grey is reminiscent of weathered sandstone and links the system to its urban context.

The lettering is in bright orange (Marabu 1208). This colour conveys information and contrasts nicely with the two background colours for easy reading. The tone is calming but also efficient and well adapted to the light and the surroundings. It has a modern touch without being excessively modish.

Signage Design

The two colours make the poles stand out. The historic centre of the city is divided into four quarters, each denoted with simple but striking signs. This coding enables the visitor to see at a glance which direction he or she needs to take.

The signs are a fun way of directing visitors around the city. The columnar appearance of the posts provides a link to the tectonic principles of the historic buildings. Some are tilted at an angle of 20° which reduces the rigidity of the system and mirrors its overall

circular unity. The oblique signs convey movement and flexibility, in stark contrast to their static vertical counterparts.

The charm of these poles lies not in any formal affinity with the architecture but in the system's rich variety of features, including text placement, different heights and colours. Like Ariadne's thread, the ribbon of yellow helps visitors orientate themselves around Dresden, and the round tips

of the posts are an unpretentious but bold addition to the urban landscape, like beacons above the clutter.

The slender form of the poles contributes to the effectiveness of the system. The information is divided into different levels, depending on the height of the poles. As the information is distributed on a convex surface, several people can read it at once.

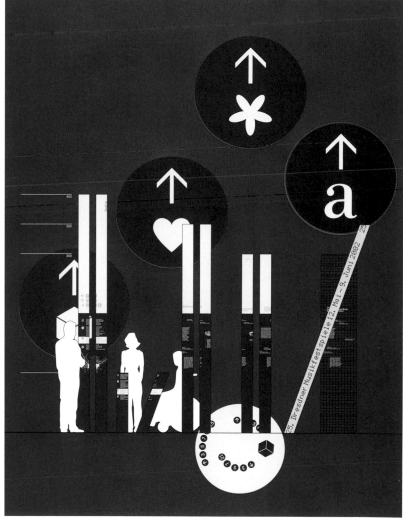

1.7 Colour
Blue

Blue is generally clients' favourite colour. They all want blue logos, signs and trademarks. However, if you choose a shade that is too dark, it sinks into obscurity. Paul Rand's blue logo for IBM is a very dark blue, but manages to stay fresh owing to its white horizontal band; the white is mixed with blue, and as a result the dark shade of blue appears lighter. In any wayfinding system, blue has to be handled very carefully because it can easily look greenish or reddish. It should never be dark, unless it is so dark that it is difficult to tell whether it is blue or black.

Wayfinding system at IFF (Industrielle Fertigung und Fabrikbetrieb), IAT (Institut für Arbeitswissenschaft und Technologiemanagement) at Stuttgart University. Thin blue bands flow through the building.

1.7 Colour
Green
Colour Tones

Service
Dark: S 0585-Y30R
Light: S 0580-Y20R

Hall 1
Dark: S 0585-Y50R
Light: S 0585-Y30R

Halls 3, 5, 7, 9
Dark: S 0585-Y80R
Light: S 0585-Y60R

Halls 2, 4, 6, 8
Dark: S 0585-Y80R
Light: S 0585-Y60R

In Europe, green is associated with emergency exits, and its use in any wayfinding system is therefore limited. The wayfinding system for the Neue Messe in Stuttgart uses a variety of bright colours, and it would have been difficult to omit green altogether from this broad spectrum. For safety reasons, green signs were only used to direct visitors to areas outside the exhibition halls. Interestingly, there is a particular form of green translucent film which, when lit from behind, makes dark green look light, and light green, dark.

Congress
Dark: S 1070-R20B
Light: S 1090-R30B

Exits
Dark: S 3065-R90B
Light: S 2065-R90B

The combination of colour tones in this system is like a kaleidoscopic pattern, both attractive and accessible. The rainbow colours enrich the architecture, subtly infiltrating your mind without you even realizing it. Blue, for example, shows the way to the exit: it takes seconds for you to make that initial connection between the two, and then you don't even have to think about it.

Outside areas
Dark: S 2075-G20Y
Light: S 2070-G30Y

VIP services
Dark: S 3060-R50B
Light: S 2060-R50B

Wayfinding system at the Neue Messe in Stuttgart. On arrival, visitors are greeted with coloured strips based on national flags. The system of colours and words creates a clear identity for Stuttgart trade fairs, and the colourful signs offer clear directions: pink for congress, blue for the exits, and red for the other halls.

The colours are taken from the NCS system, which offers a unique selection of finely balanced and differentiated shades.

In the NCS colour notation 2030-Y90R, 2030 denotes the shade – that is to say the proportion of blackness and chromaticity. This example has 20% darkness and 30% saturation. The remaining 50% is the proportion of white.

The rest of the NCS notation indicates the percentage value between two of the colours red, yellow, green or blue – in this case, 10% yellow (Y) and 90% red (R).

Colour-coded directions make it easier for visitors to find their way, enabling them to identify quickly the nature of the information they are after. This may only speed the process up by a matter of seconds, but it reduces stress and contributes to the overall efficiency of the exhibition centre.

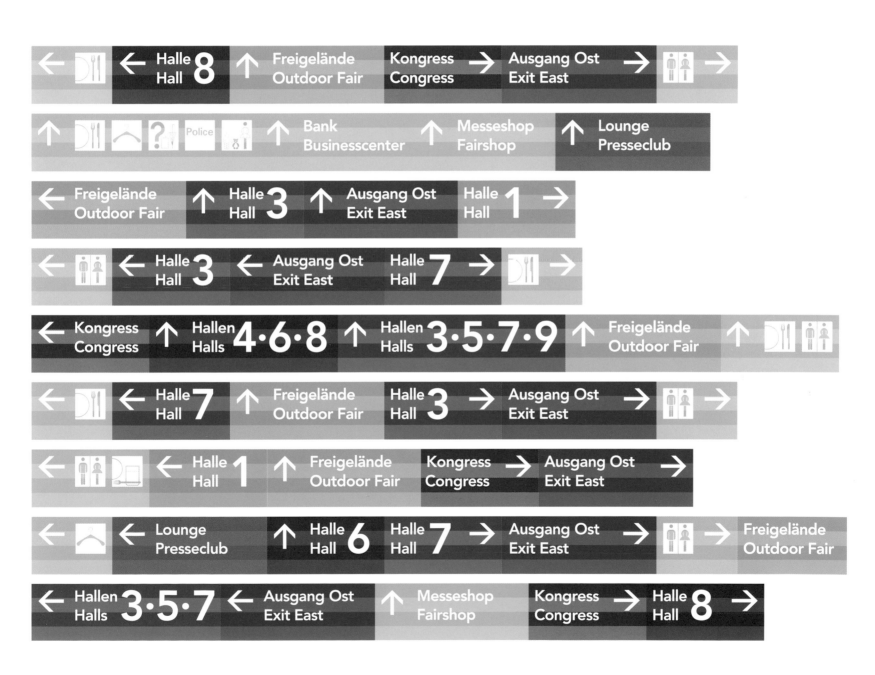

Signage Design

Floor level	Part of building	Bright yellow Dark yellow	Bright orange Dark orange	Bright red Dark red	Bright blue Dark blue	Bright green Dark green

Wayfinding system at the E.ON main administration offices in Munich. The coloured bands are distributed according to brightness: the top of the building, where there is more sunshine, is naturally lighter, and so darker colours are used. On the darker lower floors, brighter colours help to create a more cheerful atmosphere.

B.230

Revision/Rix
Dagmar Maier
Sekretariat

If someone is playing Haydn in the Mozart Room, and the Haydn Room is next door, it's small wonder that people get confused.... When an architectural complex comprises several buildings or departments, identifying rooms by name can be problematic. Corridors may join the different buildings together, and you may be aware that you have left one area and entered another through a change in the architecture or interior design, but this will not help you find your way. It therefore makes sense to differentiate between the different areas or buildings with a code. You can successfully distinguish between different areas with letters (A, B, C, and so on), and room numbers can easily be integrated: so A1 would mean room 1 in area A. If numbers are used to identify both an area and a room, the code may become confusing, particularly if a floor level also needs to be included. Likewise, too many digits make the code cumbersome; such a system should have a maximum of three digits. Conventional systems can only cope with a certain degree of complexity, after which it is necessary to go back to the drawing board.

Let's look at an example: say car park P22 has seven levels, and each level contains five sections, each with more than 100 parking lots. The code could then be P22.7B.157. You would need to write it down, or you would never find your car. There is only so much information you can pack into a coding system.

It is advisable to plan the codes right from the start of a project. If it is not done systematically, later changes are usually impossible as the codes will have been factored into all the plans to which the engineers are working. Any reformulation could prove very expense.

02.01.027

Section   Level   Room number

22.0A.248

Car park   Level   Area   Space number

Car park wayfinding system at the Neue Messe, Stuttgart. The sheer number of levels and areas inevitably leads to a confusing accumulation of codes, which are incredibly difficult to remember.

If plans for a building are laid out on a grid showing partition walls, the tiniest detail can be given a set of coordinates. This clear system avoids confusion if changes are made, without the need for complicated codes.

If you are numbering rooms in a corridor according to a code, it is best to group all even numbers on one side, and odd numbers on the other. They should also follow the same sequence, so that low even numbers are opposite low odd numbers. This makes it easier to locate whichever room you are looking for.

A, B, C or C, B, A? Where should you begin? With A? Different clients have different priorities. It makes sense for the congress hall of an exhibition centre to be designated by a 'C', but not if it is situated between areas F and E. Linguistic associations and neutral codes can be contradictory.

How should you indicate that a floor is underground? Say you opt for -1. The -1 denotes the basement, where some people have to work. However, if the building is on a slope, it might actually be at ground level. The entrance, level 0, would be further up the hill. The range of creative ideas runs from B (basement) to U (underground), but these letters are not necessarily logical nor pleasing to the eye. A code is a functional tool and should not be mishandled.

Underground car parks and high-rise buildings always pose similar problems. Graphics (pictures, pictograms etc) can be very useful here as an additional aid. Key information such as floor level should be displayed clearly and it must be easily seen from an open lift or landing. If you have to get out of the lift or open a heavy fire door to see the relevant sign, it's in the wrong place!

Pictures are easier to take in and remember than codes (see page 95). Distinguishing between levels through colour coding alone is potentially confusing, and there is a limit to how many colours you can use. Was that floor red or orange...?

Wayfinding system at Bollwerk Landesbank Baden-Württemberg, Stuttgart. It is possible to distinguish between different areas by themes: in this underground car park, each level is indicated by a colour and a portrait. The pictures were taken from the D-Mark banknotes that were in use at the time.

Wayfinding system at Bosch-Areal, Stuttgart. Different symbols were used to distinguish between the levels of the underground car park, creating a friendlier atmosphere. The shape of each symbol indicates the level: Level 1 is a circle, Level 2 is a cross (2 lines), Level 3 is a triangle (3 sides), Level 4 is a square (4 sides), and Level 5 consists of five lines.

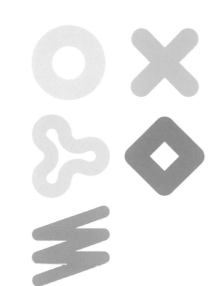

Floor levels in the Landesbank Baden-Württemberg, Pariser Platz, Stuttgart. There are nineteen storeys. The graphic coding gives each floor its own separate identity. Linked numbers corresponding to the level create an individual pattern that covers the curved walls and tells you precisely where you are.

1.8 Coding
Coding with Letters and Numbers

Wayfinding system at Stuttgart Airport. The illustrations show the two levels of the airport. The diagram below is the top level, for departures; arrivals (opposite) are directly below departures. There is a problem: in order to reach some gates (e.g. B. D and G), you have to go down from the departures level to the floor below. There is nothing particularly unusual in this, but passengers tend to assume that the linear sequence of the gates on the departures level will be an enclosed system, and thus overlook the downward flight of steps. The numerical code enables travellers to identify and follow the sequence on the main departures level more easily. Access points between the two floors are given the same numerical code.

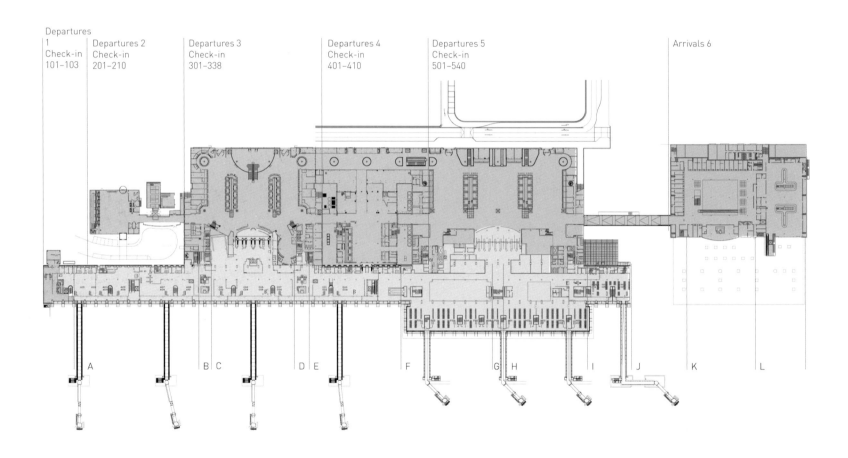

Departures 1
Check-in
101–103

Departures 2
Check-in
201–210

Departures 3
Check-in
301–338

Departures 4
Check-in
401–410

Departures 5
Check-in
501–540

Arrivals 6

A   B C   D E   F   G H   I   J   K   L

Signage Design

TERMINAL 1   ~~TERMINAL 1~~
LEVEL 3   ~~LEVEL 3~~
                   DEPARTURES 1   **DEPARTURES 1**

TERMINAL 1   ~~TERMINAL 1~~
LEVEL 2   ~~LEVEL 2~~
ARRIVALS 1   **ARRIVALS 1**   **ARRIVALS 1**

It became necessary to recode the system at Stuttgart Airport. In the previous system levels clashed with the terminal numbers. One location required three different terms to identify it, whereas the new system only needs one.

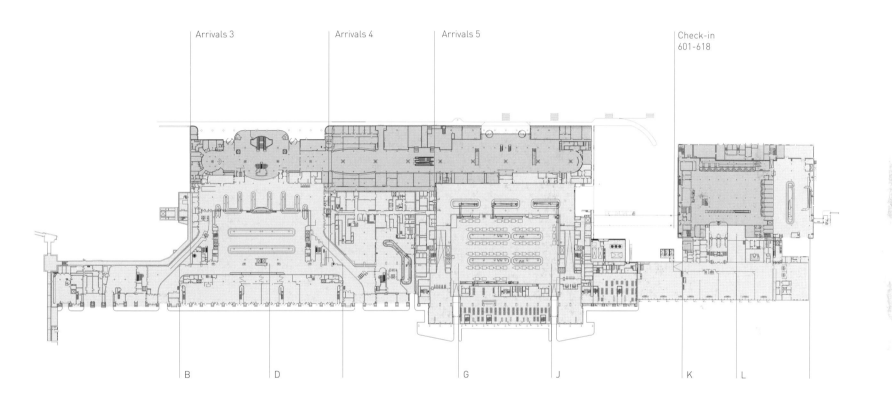

Arrivals 3   Arrivals 4   Arrivals 5   Check-in 601–618

B   D   G   J   K   L

1.8 Coding
Coding with Names

Signage Design

Wayfinding system at the executive building of HypoVereinsbank in Munich. When neutral information is conveyed, language can seem impolite and even alienating, but it can also have a familiar local association. The conference rooms take their names from streets and nearby places, and thus allow an additional element of spatial orientation. Other rooms have been given the name of the architect. Instead of 'west entrance', we have 'Salvator entrance', and one conference room is called 'the lions' den'.

1.9 Privacy and Protection

Wayfinding system at the executive building of the HypoVereinsbank in Munich. The principle of minimal intervention also applies to safety: a thin line provides a polite reminder that the room ends here. Bands of different widths are cut from film in matt silver and translucent, highly reflective silver. The gaps between them establish a regular rhythm.

In office buildings where there is a lot of glass, people need their privacy. Some employees feel that they are constantly being monitored, while others find the openness uncomfortable. In a bank, the need for privacy is all the more understandable. In order not to break the architectural flow of such spaces, it is necessary to develop graphics that will divide the glass surfaces into separate, translucent and transparent areas. A complex of colours, forms and surfaces can enrich the space.

It is necessary to protect people from colliding with glass doors and walls. This may sound a little stupid, but accidents frequently happen, especially when lighting conditions are such that the glass obstacle is hidden in darkness and the rooms behind it are well lit. We've all seen it done! It's particularly dangerous to have a glass wall near a door. If it's wide enough for a person to go through, it can cause an accident. It is therefore advisable to find ways of marking such spots. All too often this is done with unsightly dots or lines. It's possible, however, to turn this somewhat humdrum task into a genuine design feature that will fit in with the overall system and even add to it.

Large areas of glass are good to look at, but can cause problems. Depending on the amount of light, they may not be immediately visible as obstacles. Tales of broken noses and jaws are not fictional: they frequently happen. Transparent walls must be marked in such a way that they are immediately recognizable as such.

Dots and bands provide a simple way of denoting the spatial borders, but it is always nicer if the warnings become a feature in themselves, and necessity becomes a virtue. If glass walls mean a loss of privacy, graphic designs can be extended to provide an additional barrier.

Signage system at Kronen Carré, Stuttgart. Linear architectural features have been further developed to provide a graphic code. The lines are on a grid, and their length and thickness are varied. They link together the various typographical levels, and give an aesthetic slant to their protective function.

The pattern of the bands on the walls mirrors the Le Corbusier-style rhythm of the building, which is broken up by stairwells, as well as guarding against any collisions. Sometimes the shadow of a band overlaps with the silver line on the wall, which helps to break the space up into its separate sections.

These bands are also used to display information in the form of entrance codes, tenants, house numbers and so on.

á à â ä ã å
ç é è ê ë
í ì î ï ñ
ó ò ô ö õ
ú ù û ü
æ œ ÿ

Avenir Heavy,
Adrian Frutiger, 1988

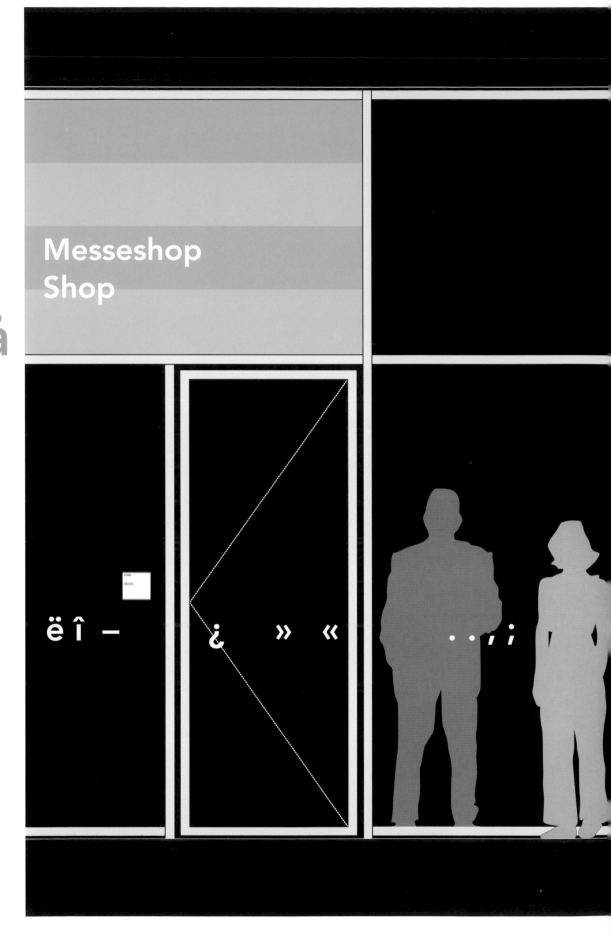

Signage Design

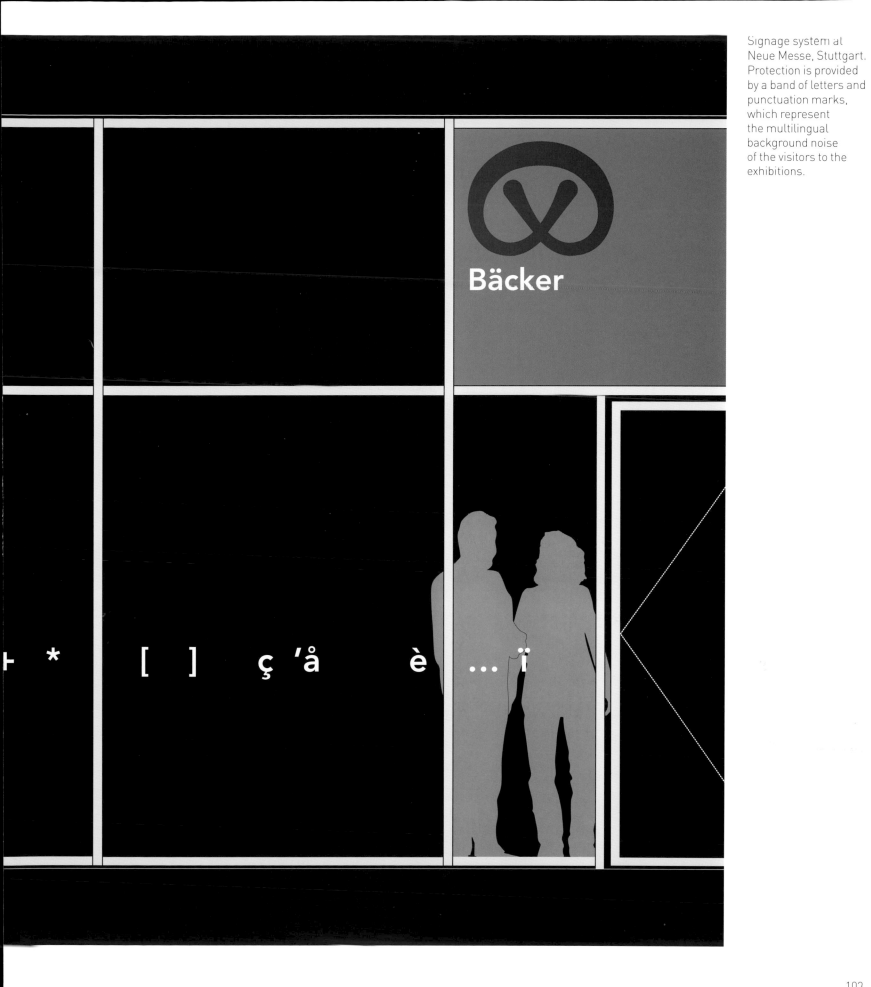

Bäcker

⊦ * [ ] ç 'å è ... ï

Signage system at Neue Messe, Stuttgart. Protection is provided by a band of letters and punctuation marks, which represent the multilingual background noise of the visitors to the exhibitions.

Signage system in the offices of Atelier West. A swirling tangle of lines marks off different areas of this office building, like a light web set against a heavy sky.

The graphic lines remain open when they are there for safety reasons, but are much thicker if privacy is needed.

Signage system at the HypoVereinsbank in Luxembourg. The building is a geometrical sculpture in concrete. The lettering, in reflective silver and grey, is neatly integrated into the concrete.

The glass surfaces are thickened and opened up by a translucent layer. The lettering and graphic elements are incorporated into a grid based on John Cage's hexagrams.

The grid is the language that facilitates the different images, and within it the type area and the signs and pictograms are laid out in a variety of rhythms.

The glass cubicles are small cash desks, where a great deal of money changes hands. Customers do not want to be observed. On the other hand, the architects favoured an open plan, and so the solution is

graphic walls: at the sensitive level where faces can be recognized, the walls are opaque, but the top and bottom of the glass and the exposed ceiling remain open, without damaging the design.

1.10 Room Identification

Rooms need to be identifiable. A caretaker has to know exactly which room has a leaking tap. Some rooms are easy, and can be labelled and numbered with transfer tape, although when doors are repainted, the lettering is often taken off and not replaced. This can leave ugly lumps and bumps as the old paint shows up through the new. Rooms where people work require door plates. Identification has to be flexible as the occupants may change. The graphic designer will plan the layout and the typography, and the client can then implement the system himself.

There are many such systems on the market, all of them functional, but few are nice to look at. Our frustration at this situation prompted us to design a door plate that can be used without any special tools and also satisfies our artistic aspirations – as well as those of our architects and clients.

The Sero Flex is a mass-produced system for identifying rooms. The information is displayed on a sheet of white paper which can be printed with any conventional office printer. The sheet is placed between a wall fixture of silver anodized aluminium and a matt pane of acrylic glass, held together by a dovetail joint. A polished steel clip stops the glass from slipping, and can be removed with a magnet. The lower section of the dovetail also holds the sheet in place, even without the acrylic glass cover. The wall fixture can also be delivered in other anodized colours. The package includes software with which it is possible to vary the typographical design of the insert. The straightforward design enables this system to fit into any architectural context, and the assembly can be linear, horizontal or vertical.

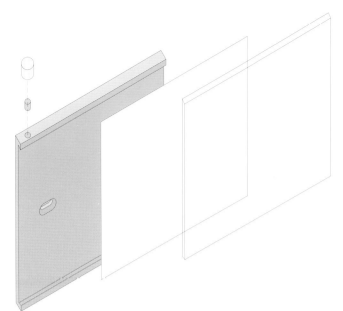

'I used to be *oriental* until I was told that the politically correct term is Asian—now I have become *dis-oriented*.' www.dis-oriented.com

The verb 'orient' or 'orientate' is derived, via Old French, from the Latin *oriri*, 'to rise', referring to the sun rising in the east. The French verb *orienter* originally meant to position towards the east, but the meaning gradually expanded to embrace all directions. Nowadays, when we orientate ourselves, we try to find out either where we are, or where we need to go.

In this chapter, we shall be giving a rough guide to the planning process in ten steps. A detailed description would be beyond the scope of this book, but these ten stages will offer some assistance in how to go about structuring a project.

Step 1: the contract. A contract is essential to the establishment of a good relationship between client and designer. It details what is expected of the designer. With any major signage system, the client has a right to expect all aspects of the graphic work to be included in the deal. This is also in the interests of the designer. The examples given in this book show that projects that supply a complete and efficient graphic system are able to give the place an identity, transform the nature of the areas they occupy, and of course provide wayfinding.

With smaller, simpler projects it often makes sense to take a slightly different approach. For instance, individual items can be described and priced (e.g. Item 1: door identification; Item 2: company flag...). It is advisable to set a flat fee for the commission. This means that the designer must supply everything that is relevant to the information being conveyed, which may mean that certain items that the client considers necessary may in fact be dropped. Say, for instance, the client wants a distinctive sign that can be seen from a distance; he may have originally envisaged the firm's name on the roof, but the designer may choose something completely different, like a flag. The commission will have been fulfilled by the flag (or its equivalent). Negotiating a flat fee has the advantage that there is no need for detailed itemization, which is often not possible when the contract is initially awarded, because the designer has not yet been able to tackle the task directly. The disadvantage for the client, however, is that he needs to put all his trust in the judgment and integrity of the designer. The concern is whether it will all be done properly. To a degree, you can set his mind at rest by describing all the possible concepts, but you must also make it clear that they will not all come to fruition as this will depend on the ultimate design.

In our hypothetical project, the different planning stages can be linked to advance payments. For example, we have the draft, the actual design, a list of functions to be fulfilled, allocation of work, supervision and monitoring of the site. The cost of the presentation must be covered by the fee, and it is advisable to negotiate a fixed sum for expenses.

The basis of good cooperation is the contract. It must work for both parties. If there are no disagreements, you may not need to refer to it, but once you have it, there should be no room for disagreement. If there is a conflict, the contract will settle it, because terms have already been agreed.

The contract is therefore the foundation of every project, creating the right attitude and atmosphere from the start.

Step 2: obtaining information. Once the contract has been finalized, it is essential to have a plan of the building. The architect will supply the details, but before he does so, you should ask him to remove or black out irrelevant information. If he refuses – and he is under no obligation to do this – you will have to do it yourself, which involves a lot of work but has to be done. It makes the plan clearer, it looks better, and the amount of data is significantly reduced. On the plan you will need the following: ground plans, cross-sections and general views on a scale of 1:100; in larger buildings, 1:200; all walls that are relevant to the graphic design, 1:50; plan of the site, 1:500. Individual details should be on a scale of 1:20, 1:10, or in some cases 1:1.

The designer needs an intimate knowledge of the building and all its functions. The project leader from the architects' firm or the client himself should explain the necessary directions, exits and entrances, uses, and the exact nature of the location (e.g. situated on River X, the riverbank slopes and is covered in weeping willows). Even the tiniest, seemingly unimportant details may have a bearing on the design. The system must be infallible. Once you are familiar with all the facts, you can either incorporate them or forget about them, but first you must know them.

Wayfinding system at the Bucerius Law School in Hamburg. With so much information displayed, structured typography is essential.

What information do you need to show, and where? Which departments and names should be displayed? What is the hierarchy of information, and how flexible should the system be? The level of information required is an important factor in the design. A display board detailing seven institutes, thirteen professors, lecture rooms, library, WC etc can only be made effective by typographical means: indentations, different fonts and spacing will all help to differentiate between the masses of information (see illustration on the right).

It is also important to have all the technical and architectural data. How are the walls, floors and ceilings structured? Can you drill holes into them? Is there underfloor heating? The zigzag form of the information displays in the Augsburg state insurance building (opposite, top left) was due to underfloor heating. The construction of sharp-edged, welded aluminium is so heavy that it cannot be moved, and its three-dimensional form prevents it from being tipped over, even though it is not actually fixed to the floor.

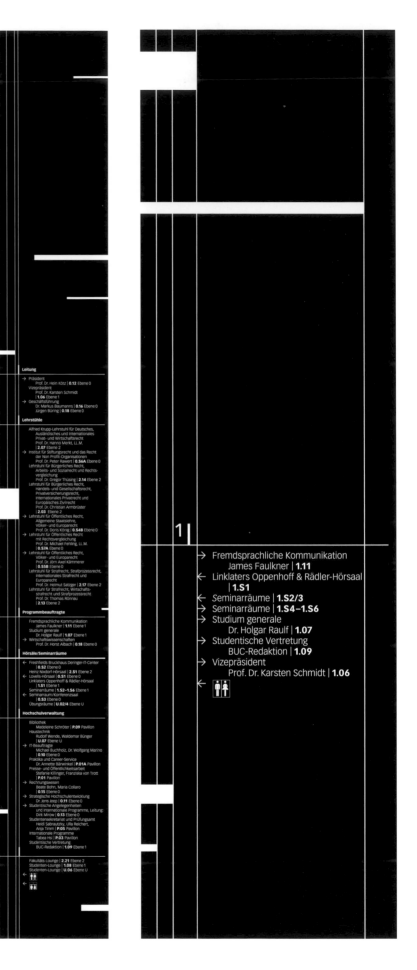

Wayfinding system
at the state insurance
building in Augsburg.
The existing structure
determined the jagged
form of the signs:
owing to underfloor
heating, they couldn't
be fixed to the floor.

Wayfinding system
at the state insurance
building in Augsburg.
The existing structure
determined the jagged
form of the signs:
owing to underfloor
heating, they couldn't
be fixed to the floor.

295 | 296
297 | 298
299 | 300
301 | 302
303 | 304
305 | 306

Wayfinding system
at Stuttgart Airport.
The signs here are
colour-coded: red
for flight information,
black for infrastructure
and white for retail.
The numbers help
to synchronize signs
and content and to
pinpoint them in the
ground plan.

Step 3: preliminary design. All the data is gathered
together on a site or ground plan. At every point
where information is needed, there has to be a
directional sign. Normally, there should be a general
information board at the entrance, indicating the way
to particular areas. Wherever people have to decide
whether to go left, right, up, down or straight on, a
new sign must be marked on the plan.

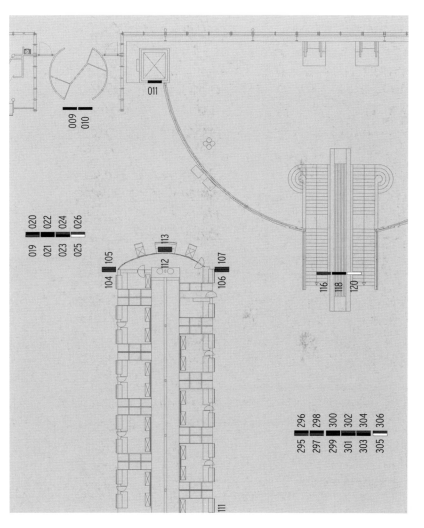

2.4 Design

In any design, there are always certain elements you can draw on to help you. The nature of the business is one factor (see E.ON on pages 288–93, for example), and the structure of the building or the budget naturally also play a part. The wayfinding system for a spa house in Bad Brambach (above) had a restricted budget, which meant carrying out the work at the simplest possible level. The solution was to lay out all directions without a rigid format, produce them on transfer tape, and then stick them to existing surfaces.

The preliminary design should be shown to the client, but as the graphic designer's work intrudes on that of the architect and may infringe his copyright, it is important to reach an agreement with him first. If he does not approve, you can go no further. If he has reservations, these must be taken seriously. Consultation with the architect should be seen as something positive. There are, however, some firms that will not agree to any major graphic intrusion on their work, but prefer the graphics to be conventional and unobtrusive. There are also first-class architects who welcome collaboration with

artists, engineers and communications designers as an enrichment of their work. If the architecture is poor quality, it will be difficult to prevent the design from suffering too, since the graphic element will always be seen in the overall context.

The preliminary design shows the basic idea. This must be functional but also achievable within the constraints of the budget. If no budget has been set, an estimate must be supplied with the preliminary plan.

The plan must fix, detail and describe the following parts of the system:

• typographical system and type area

• modular layout and dimensions

• system of signs and pictograms

• system of surfaces and colours

• coding system for sections, floor levels and rooms

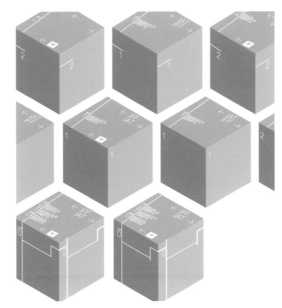 

Step 4: design. After the presentation of the preliminary design, the client, users or architect will probably want changes. These may be connected with the function or with the aesthetic appearance of the system. The customer is always right. He must like the ideas, and there have been many cases in which poor designs have resulted in the client quite rightly demanding a number of changes or even a different programme. If changes are necessary in terms of the suitability or quality of the plan, the new designs must naturally fall in line with the agreed budget – in other words, revisions and alternatives must be carried out without any additional cost. However, if the client turns nasty, or tries to impose a solution, it is worth considering whether the contract should be terminated. If the client or architect has doubts about the proposal, even though the designer is convinced of its quality, it can still be worked on and revised, as the projects illustrated above show.

The design must present functional solutions to all problems. Each part of the system has to be worked out and tested for each application. The design must also be accompanied by a statement of cost, based on the quantity required. Once the client has agreed to the design, planning can begin for the production and construction of the various installations. If construction work is to be a major undertaking, structural engineers must be brought on board, and in such cases the designer's tender must specify that the structural work and any prototypes will be paid for separately.

Competition for visual identity and wayfinding system, German Maritime Museum, Bremerhaven. The dominant symbol is the banner fluttering cheerfully in the breeze. It makes reference to a great naval tradition: the transatlantic race. The Blue Riband, awarded to the ship with the fastest record, is used here for a variety of functions. An easily recognizable thread that runs throughout the museum, it helps visitors to find their way and gives them all the information they need. After you have exhausted everything there is to see, the Blue Riband will show you out or, better still, the way to the café. Outside the museum building, you are welcomed by swirling ribbons on masts, telling you that this place is special.

Some of the examples shown here and on the following pages are taken from competition entries and designs. The more precise your proposal is, the greater your chance of winning over clients and architects. Precise graphic representation is also the best means of testing a project. The drawings can be used later as the basis for the final plan and also to explain the costing to the client.

Signage Planning

Presentations of preliminary sketches and final designs should always be to scale. Drawings that contain people, trees, cars etc will give a better idea of the scale. Axonometric drawing and general views can also be useful in conveying an overall impression.

Even if a client rejects a good idea, the work is never wasted. It hides itself away in the unconscious and then one day – hopefully at the right time – suddenly resurfaces for another project.

Competition for visual identity and wayfinding system for Stihl Gallery, Waiblingen/ Kunstschule Unteres Remstal. So as not to interfere with the shimmering lightness of the façade, translucent poles are erected outside to mark the identity of the buildings. These coloured perpendicular structures echo the vertical lines of the façade and are internally lit. The poles are strategically positioned outside the two buildings, and the lettering clearly identifies them as a gallery and a school. They also carry information about various events, and written texts and posters can be placed on them diagonally. Day and night, these yellow and red masts emit an artistic radiance.

Competition for wayfinding system, Pappas Motor Company, Salzburg. The client understandably wanted to show off the architecture as well as the cars, which was the determining factor. The design was incorporated into the architect's uncluttered drawings, which were to scale. This enabled those involved to test the suitability of the proposal and present the ideas vividly.

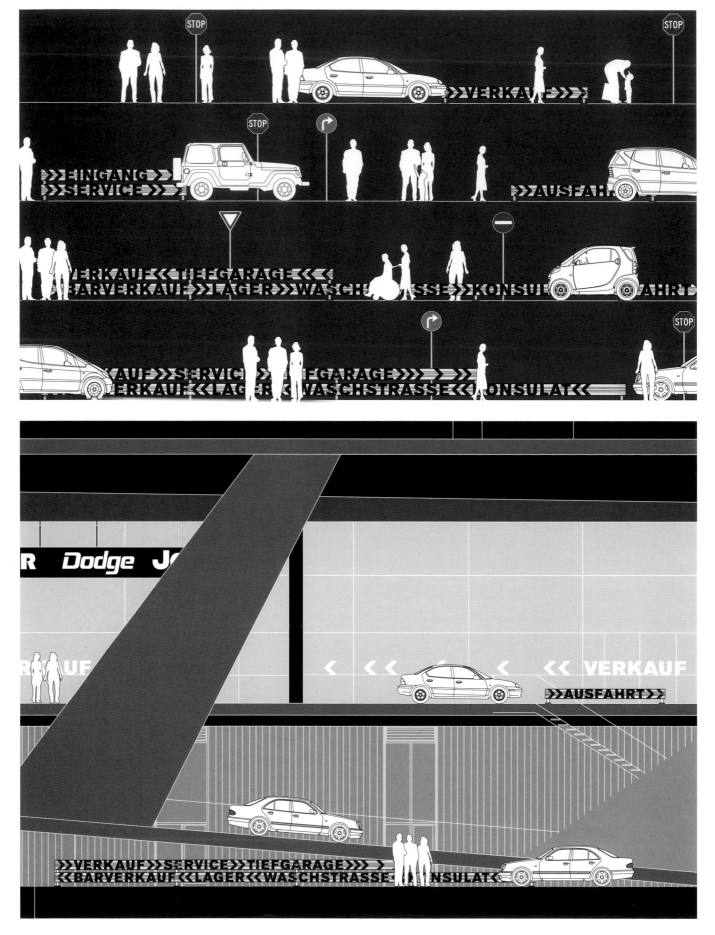

Competition for the Le Corbusier Museum and wayfinding system for the Weissenhof-siedlung in Stuttgart, in collaboration with the architect Uwe Münzing. The construction, made of cubes, is sensitively integrated into its hill setting. It is adorned with white and red spheres: the small white ones show the name of the architect and the date of construction, and stand outside the buildings that have been preserved or destroyed. The larger red spheres give an overview of the whole site. The simple spherical element links up with the formal language of the cubes, but keeps its distance and should be viewed as an accessory.

119

Dimetric, isometric and trimetric projections are useful ways of representing three-dimensional objects in two dimensions. They are all axonometric. In isometric projections the three axes of space appear equally foreshortened; in dimetric projections, two of the three appear equally foreshortened; and in trimetric projections, all three appear unequally foreshortened. The Cavalier perspective is an alternative method, but only attempts to convey a sense of depth.

The choice of angle will depend on the object. In some cases, representations are impossible to understand; in the isometric projection of a cube, two points coincide. Here the Cavalier perspective would be a better choice.

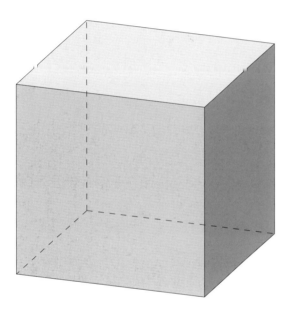

Dimetric: 7⁰/42⁰
Foreshortening factor
(width, height, depth):
1:1, 1:1, 1:2

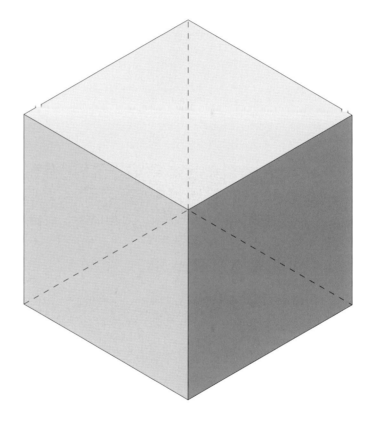

Isometric: 30⁰/30⁰
Foreshortening factor
(width, height, depth):
1:1, 1:1, 1:1

Spatial representation helps to convey the ideas behind the design. Geometrical axonometries are preferable to perspective as they give a more accurate and often a more attractive impression of the object.

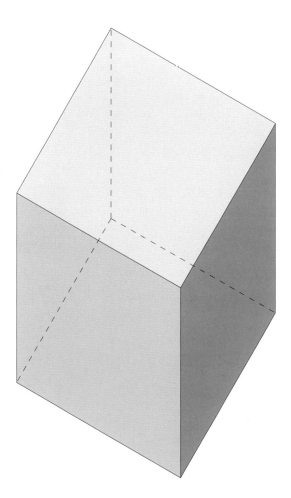

Cavalier: 30⁰/30⁰
Foreshortening factor
(width, height, depth):
1:1, 1:1, 1:1

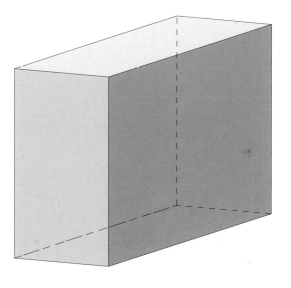

Trimetric: 5⁰/18⁰
Foreshortening factor
(width, height, depth):
1:2, 1:1, 1:9/10

2.5 Construction, Work Plan and Prototypes

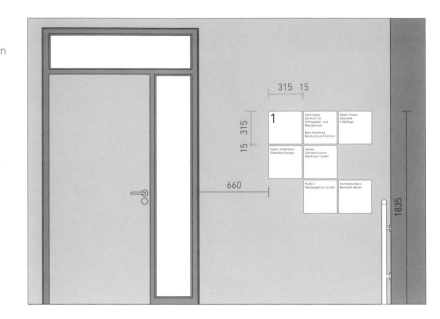

Step 5: construction, work plan and prototypes. All the details and installations must be drawn to scale on the plan. This is the basis on which the whole system will be constructed, and so it is essential to test beforehand the technical feasibility, the maintenance requirements, the cost, and every single application of the system. The required quantities must be accurately listed.

How the system is to be constructed is a vital component of the design. It has to be tested according to all the demands that will be made on it, and these will vary considerably according to the nature of the project. For example, in a public area, the surfaces must be vandal-proof. Flexibility is essential, however much you may want something done in a particular way. You must be realistic about how affordable it will be. Standard inscriptions made up of individual letters on transfer tape are not always practical, because they are often easily removable. If there are a lot of items requiring identical inscriptions, silkscreen printing may be more economical. Illuminated signs intended to last for, say, five years should be tested for economical use of energy and for maintenance requirements. When we designed the wayfinding system at Stuttgart Airport, we decided that the use of long-life, energy-saving LEDs (light-emitting diodes), which are still relatively expensive, would not be economical over this period. The conventional solution, using T5 fluorescent tubes, has higher maintenance costs because they have a far shorter life than LEDs and consume more energy. However, LEDs only have a lifespan of about ten years, and any short-term saving is therefore completely wiped out.

The designs must first be tested out with mock-ups, and tenders are invited for the manufacture of prototypes. The knowledge gained from these is then noted and put to use in the final phase. Prototypes are fully functioning mock-ups, made with the authentic materials and surface coatings. They will show whether, for instance, matt paint is better suited than glossy (though glossy is easier to maintain), or whether particular shapes and forms will reinforce or detract from the aesthetic impact of the system. Prototypes are developed in collaboration with outside companies, who are paid separately for their work. There is then a model on which bidding companies can base their tender for the system itself. Even for smaller projects, a 1:1 mock-up should be produced, but if this is too expensive, a sample section will have to do.

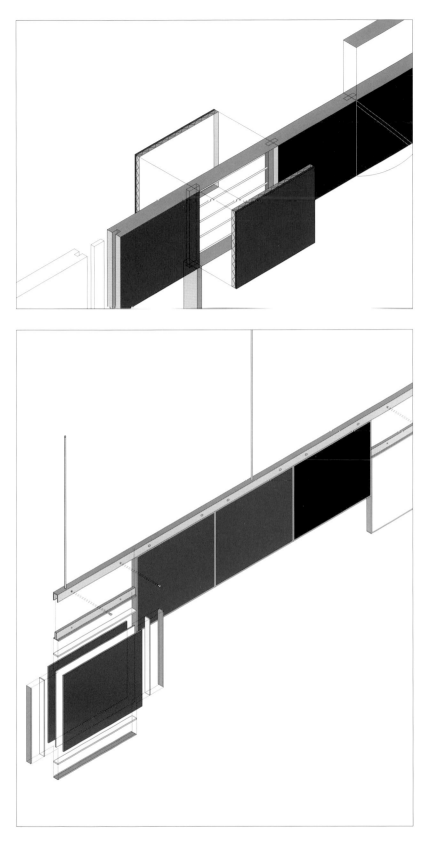

Wayfinding system
at Stuttgart Airport.
Constructional
drawings illustrating
alternative fitments
for fluorescent tubes
(above) and LEDs
(below).

The invitation to submit tenders for the prototype will contain drawings that have already been tested by a structural engineer. By this time, an agreement will also have been reached with the architect about how these new designs are to be integrated into his work. If information cannot be attached directly to existing surfaces, there are few systems that can function without the introduction of some new structure. Wayfinding systems are a three-dimensional means of communication, and the structural elements must be of the same quality as the graphics, or vice versa. Sadly there are many instances where this isn't the case, and where one lets the other down, which takes its toll on the whole system. It makes sense always to work with a company of interior designers or architects, even as early as the preliminary design phase. By collaborating in this way, you can involve such companies right from the start in the process of development. This may, of course, be a risky investment for the firms involved, but it can sometimes pay dividends when it comes to the tenders stage.

2.6 Things to Be Done
2.7 Tenders and Award of Contract

Wayfinding system at the Alsterdorf Evangelical Foundation medical centre. The signs are milled plastic. The detailed spec is just one of many tasks in the 'to do' list, as shown in the text below. A scale plan of how the signs are to be positioned is on page 122.

Step 6: things to be done. This list contains details of all the items a designer will have to supply. In order for the bidder to do a precise costing, the designer must first provide a spec breaking down the project to the finest detail – preferably accompanied by drawings providing a clear overview. Important components of this list include expectations and timing of the work, font usage (with special attention to licence requirements), and how the specification to be handed over (e.g. Mac, A1 format etc). The colour system must also be detailed (NCS, RAL etc), along with any required mock-ups, which must be approved by the client and/or the planning department. If the signwriter needs to produce lettering in a specific font on transfer tape, he must have the necessary licence. With pictograms, it is the client who must obtain the licence for the quantity and the duration he requires. If a font is already in use by the company, an extra licence is not needed.

Sample text inviting tenders for sign placing (illustrations above and opposite): plastic signs 150/150/20 mm in Ureol, one viewing side milled with sharp edge, four sides polished before milling, all surfaces polished. Surfaces and edges must be absolutely clean and level, with no scratches or traces of work or production processes. Back with four keyholes, wall sides with four flat-head screws and appropriate plugs (for concrete). Prepaint Ureol with plastic bonding primer. Monochrome paint (white or silver) in three stages: 1) base; 2) two layers of two-component auto-acrylic (precise colour given); 3) after drying, paint with clear-matt auto-clear. The paint must be able to take silkscreen and film, and be UV- and weatherproof. No powder-coating (see layout pp. 1, 4-9, drawing No. 1). Supply and assemble drill template, same milling for all 16 parts. Lettering on high-quality cast film silver or white (e.g. Scotch 3M 100-20 or similar value). Supply and fit 23 pieces of white-based silver lettering.

Scale drawing for
series production
of signs.

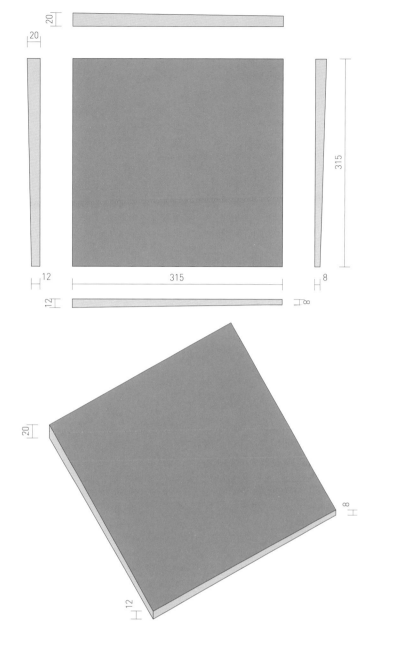

Step 7: tenders and award of contract. The list
detailed opposite forms the basis for tenders. The
invitation can be advertised publicly, or it may be
offered directly to a number of bidders.

The list is subject to a deadline by which all tenders
must be submitted. These are then evaluated, which
entails checking each item for possible errors and
anomalies (e.g. excessively high or low prices). Major
discrepancies in the costing could indicate that the
requirements have not been properly understood or
that there has been a mistake in the specifications.
It is the job of the planning department to point
such matters out and, if necessary, to provide
explanations. Prices are compared, and a shortlist
drawn up. The competitors are then invited one after
another to give their presentations. This is also an
opportunity to discuss technical alternatives that
may not have been in the original plans. When all the
presentations and negotiations are finished, the firm
that has been awarded the contract receives written
confirmation from the client.

The human brain is a strange instrument. When you see a glass door with the word 'push' on the front and 'pull' on the back, the combination is confusing, because through the glass you can see the mirror image of 'pull' at the same time that you are being told to 'push'.

During the design phase, there are so many important things to consider that some may well be forgotten. This isn't a disaster but may entail extra expense. Signwriters don't like having to put things right afterwards. Even comparatively trivial matters like 'push/pull' should be included in the list of things to be done.

Step 8: handover of specification. Once the signwriter has been appointed, the project and its particular features are discussed with him. The handover of the spec is governed by a schedule, but it is advisable to make mock-ups initially, so that they can be tested before series production begins. The handover of the final plans is accompanied by a layout that makes it clear to the signwriter whereabouts on the ground plan, cross-sectional diagram or wall the signs are to be located. It sometimes happens that the spec itself is inaccurate and the drawing is correct. A good supplier will notice this and can prevent errors in production. The precise scale drawing will also help the signwriter or whoever installs the signs, and each position will have a drawing. In a large building, recurrent factors must be systematically described – for example, the top of a door plate must always be located at a height of 145 cm and at a distance of 40 mm from the frame, on the handle side of the door. However, it may turn out that there is a fire alarm or some other piece of apparatus in this precise spot. This is where the site manager has to step in.

Step 9: on-site management. On the site, the project has to be supervised. There is always the possibility that problems to do with the plans or the building itself may arise. It is therefore essential that a site manager is present on the spot, preferably the project manager who will be familiar with all aspects of the design.

Step 10: completion. When the work is completed, there is a formal inspection carried out by the client, the signwriter and the planner. This is when any missing items or deficiencies are noted, and an agreement is reached on a date by which they must be rectified. After all parties have signed this document, the signwriter and the planner have a right to be paid most of their outstanding fees, on condition that the deficiencies are not too serious. Generally, they will receive 90% of their fees at this stage. The remaining 10% will be due as soon as the final corrections have been made. The signwriter will then draw up a closing invoice, which will be checked by the planners. If it has been agreed beforehand that all work should be documented, the papers must be handed over to the client before the final invoice is settled.

Signage Planning

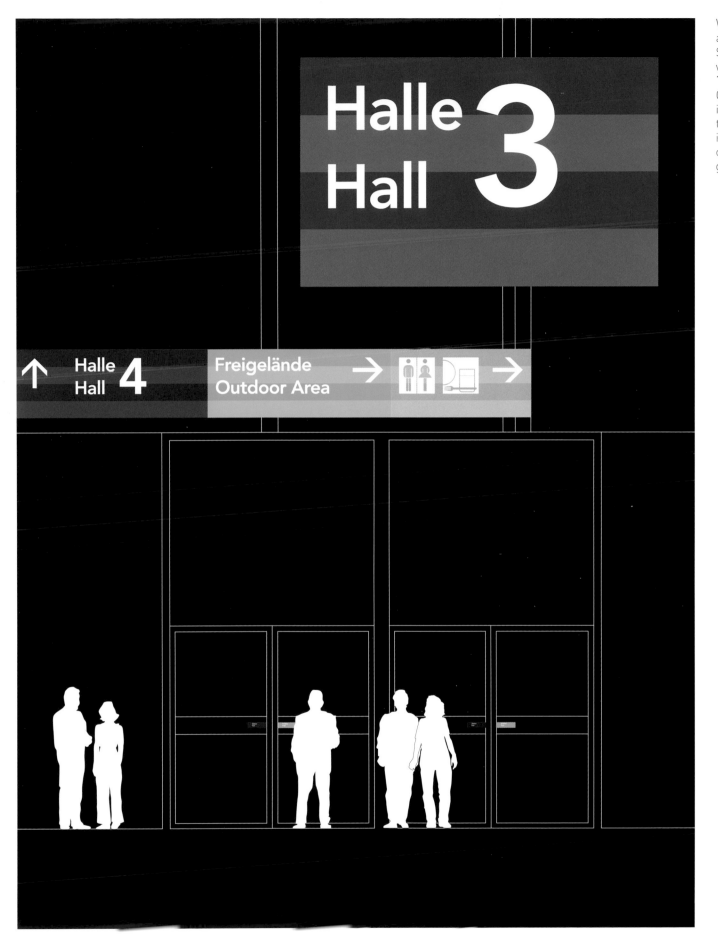

Wayfinding system at the Neue Messe, Stuttgart. 'Push' is in white on green, and 'pull' is in white on red. Coloured film is used in order to block out the contradictory instruction on the other side of the glass door.

'To orient oneself, in the proper sense of the word, means to use a given direction – and we divide the horizon into four of these – in order to find others, and in particular that of sunrise.... I can now extend this geographical concept of the process of orientation to signify any kind of orientation within a given space, i.e. orientation in a purely mathematical sense.... Finally, I can extend this concept even further if I equate it with the ability to orientate oneself not just in space, i.e. mathematically, but also in thought, i.e. logically.'
Immanuel Kant

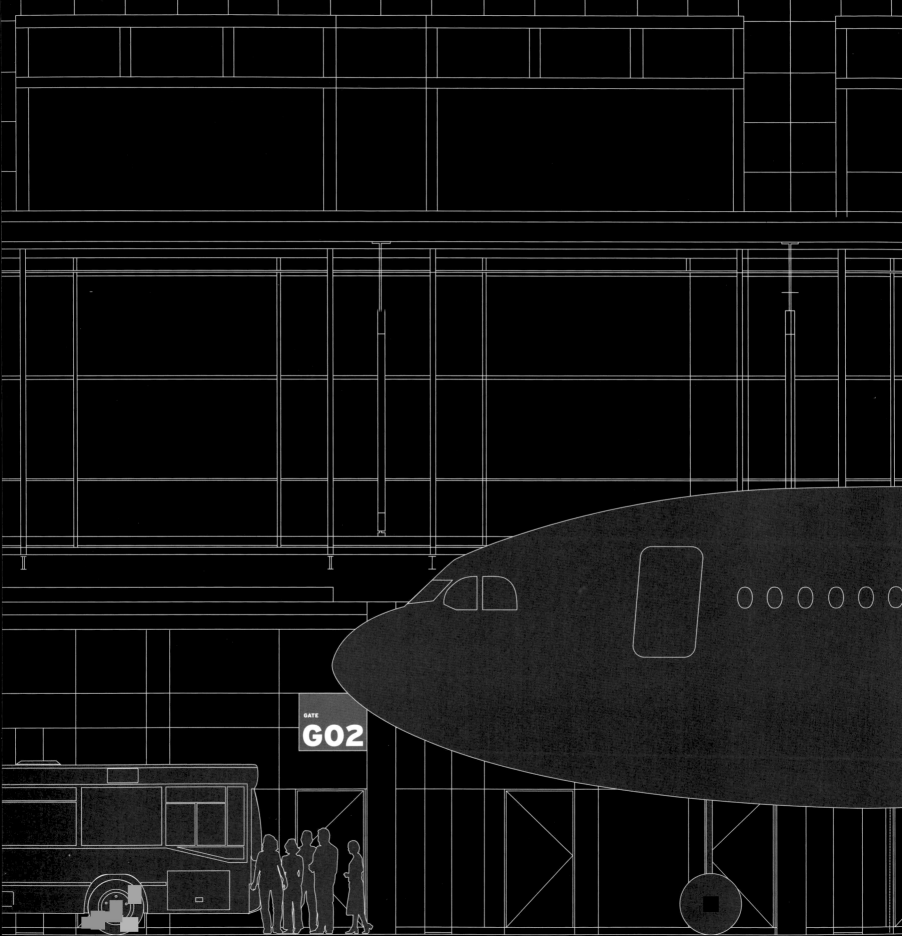

GATE
G02

Advertisements cry out: 'Buy me!' The notice board announces: 'A25'! The pulse throbs: Your heart has something to tell you. The clock warns: 'You're late!' The sign laughs: 'Over here, over there', and now 'straight on'. White on red, plain as can be, so clear and so large that even without your glasses, which you forgot in the rush, you can still read it.

Düsseldorf International Airport
Germany
1996
MetaDesign

A fire at Düsseldorf Airport in April 1996 resulted in the design of a completely new information and wayfinding system. At the centre of the new concept is a systematic prioritization of information for passengers. This is the most important aspect of the new design, together with the positioning of the signs.

Passengers are all too familiar with the following scenario: your flight was an hour late coming in, and now you have five minutes to find the gate for your connection. But where is A72? In order for this question to be answered swiftly and spontaneously, it is essential that flight and security information should be clearly distinguishable from services.

Primary signs are in green and generally mounted higher up, while secondary signs (e.g. for baby changing facilities, lifts, lounges etc) are in grey and at a lower level.

MbHg61

FF Info Display Book Normal
Erik Spiekermann and
Ole Schäfer, 1996

The lettering is in white on a green or grey background. For reflected light, the style used is Book, and on internally illuminated signs it's Normal.

3M 10280
Primary information

3M 10288
Secondary information

3M 3630-015
Arrows and pictograms

↑ ✈ **Abflug / Departures**
ℹ **Information**

A 84 ✈ →

✈ **Abflug / Departures**

Directional pictograms in white are positioned to the left or right of a yellow arrow box, depending on the direction. If there are several pieces of information linked to a single direction, the arrow only appears once, and the pictograms are set directly below one another. If a pictogram denotes a place, it has a yellow background.

German and English are divided by an oblique stroke, or appear on separate lines set close together.

The layout of the information begins, in accordance with our reading practice, in the top left-hand corner. The sequence of directions and relevant information is based on the hierarchy of arrows shown, which are positioned in such a way as to lead the visitor through the information in the logical order.

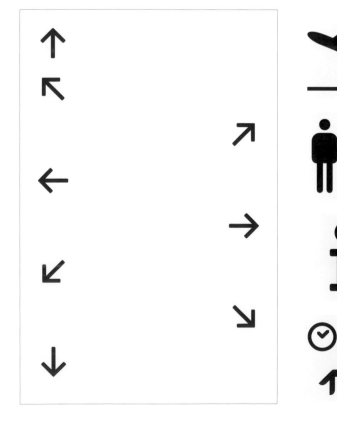

The information is prioritized, with the most urgent information at the forefront. The clear design gives passengers a greater sense of security, helping them to feel more at ease in the often chaotic airport environment.

135

The technical design of illuminated signs is such that they can be lit with simple but effective reflectors and a single fluorescent tube. The reflectors are made of white acrylic glass, and the whole sign is covered with translucent film. This particular colour was developed exclusively for Düsseldorf Airport. Only the lettering and the pictograms are left uncovered and are illuminated.

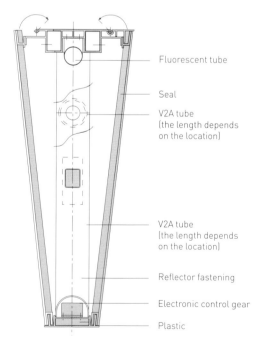

Fluorescent tube

Seal

V2A tube
(the length depends on the location)

V2A tube
(the length depends on the location)

Reflector fastening

Electronic control gear

Plastic

Airports
Düsseldorf International Airport

1600 × 420

↑ ◤ Abflug / Departures
ℹ Information
A 84 ▶ →

Abflug / Departures ▶ ↑
Information ℹ
← ◤ A 84

↑ ◤ Abflug / Departures
ℹ Information
A 84 ▶ →

1300 × 420

↑ ◤ Abflug / Departures
ℹ Information

Abflug / Departures ▶ ↑
Information ℹ

↑ ◤ Abflug / Departures
ℹ Information

1070 × 420

↑ ◤ Abflug
Departures

Abflug ▶ ↑
Departures

↑ ◤ Abflug
Departures

820 × 420

↑ ◤ A 80

A 80 ▶ ↑

↑ ◤ A 80

Small suspended signs for
secondary information and
for low ceilings

Large pylon for secondary
information 650 x 2260

500 × 300

← ♂♀ ♿

↑ ♀♀ Toiletten
Toilets
Wickelraum
Baby Room
Wartebereich
Waiting Area
Bar

820 × 300

♿ ↑
← ♂♀

1070 × 300

↑ ◤ Abflug
Departures

← ♿ Wartebereich
Waiting Area

The 120 grid is divided
into 12 x 12 units per
module

Module: 120 x 120 mm
Unit: 10 x 10 mm
Pictograms:
100 x 100 mm

Height of lettering:
7 units measured by
the ascenders of the
lower-case letters

Space between
pictograms: 2 units
Space between
pictogram and text:
3 units

The 72 grid is divided
into 12 x 12 units per
module

Module: 72 x 72 mm
Unit: 6 x 6 mm
Pictogram:
60 x 60 mm

Height of lettering:
7 units measured by
the ascenders of the
lower-case letters

Space between
pictograms: 2 units
Space between
pictogram and text:
3 units

The 50 grid is divided
into 10 x 10 units per
module

Module: 50 x 50 mm
Unit: 5 x 5 mm
Pictograms:
40 x 40 mm

Height of lettering:
5.5 units measured by
the ascenders of the
lower-case letters

Space between
pictograms: 2 units
Space between
pictogram and text:
2 units

Small pylon
420 x 1700

Cologne/Bonn Airport
Terminals 1 and 2, Car Parks 2 and 3
Germany
2004
Designgruppe Flath & Frank

The guiding principle behind the design was to make complex airport information as accessible as possible to passengers by organizing it selectively. Everything of direct relevance to flights is treated as primary information, and is made to stand out from services etc (secondary information).

This is achieved by differentiating between the colour, density and quantity of information, size of letters and signs, and prioritization in the layout. The technical implementation of the designs took into account the architectural surroundings, particularly the lighting conditions created by the large amount of glass. As this high degree of transparency increases the number of visual influences, important information needs to be kept to a minimum. The system is based on a few different elements, a clear layout, and simple but striking surfaces and formats. The surfaces of the signs are mainly non-reflective. Clear and consistent signs always make it easier for people to find their way around any building.

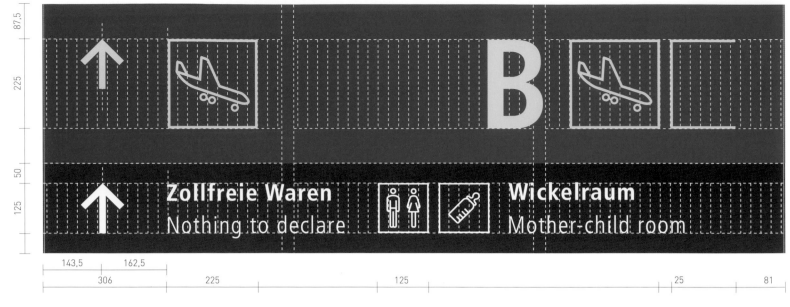

Blue background with yellow typography for primary information, and black background with white lettering for secondary information. Within this system, it is easy to incorporate signs in other colours that do not clash – e.g. the Federal Railways logo, suburban railways and parking.

Blue: Scotchcal 3M
3630-VT 1228

Yellow: Röhm Plexiglas
Yellow 304

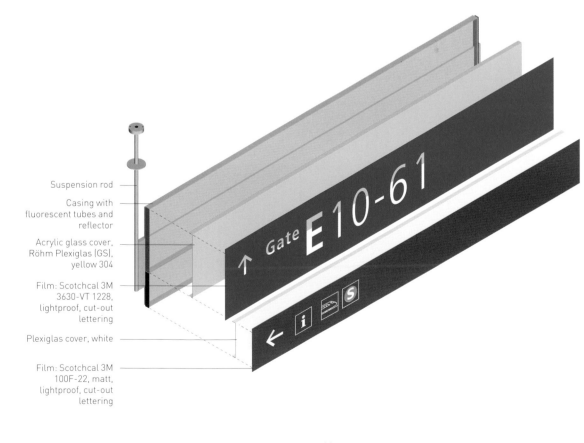

Suspension rod

Casing with
fluorescent tubes and
reflector

Acrylic glass cover,
Röhm Plexiglas (GS),
yellow 304

Film: Scotchcal 3M
3630-VT 1228,
lightproof, cut-out
lettering

Plexiglas cover, white

Film: Scotchcal 3M
100F-22, matt,
lightproof, cut-out
lettering

The information signs are luminous but not flat, in order to prevent glare. The back lighting of letters and signs is so discreet that you don't even notice the source of the light. This helps to make the signs consistently readable in all lighting conditions. They are made of aluminium and acrylic glass, and the surfaces are covered with matt, anti-reflection film.

New pictograms were designed especially for this project, using conventional international signs. The objective was to create maximum homogeneity between letters and pictograms. Confronting people with completely new symbols should be avoided.

Bce 123
Bce 123

Frutiger 67 Condensed Bold
and Frutiger 47 Condensed
Light, Adrian Frutiger, 1976

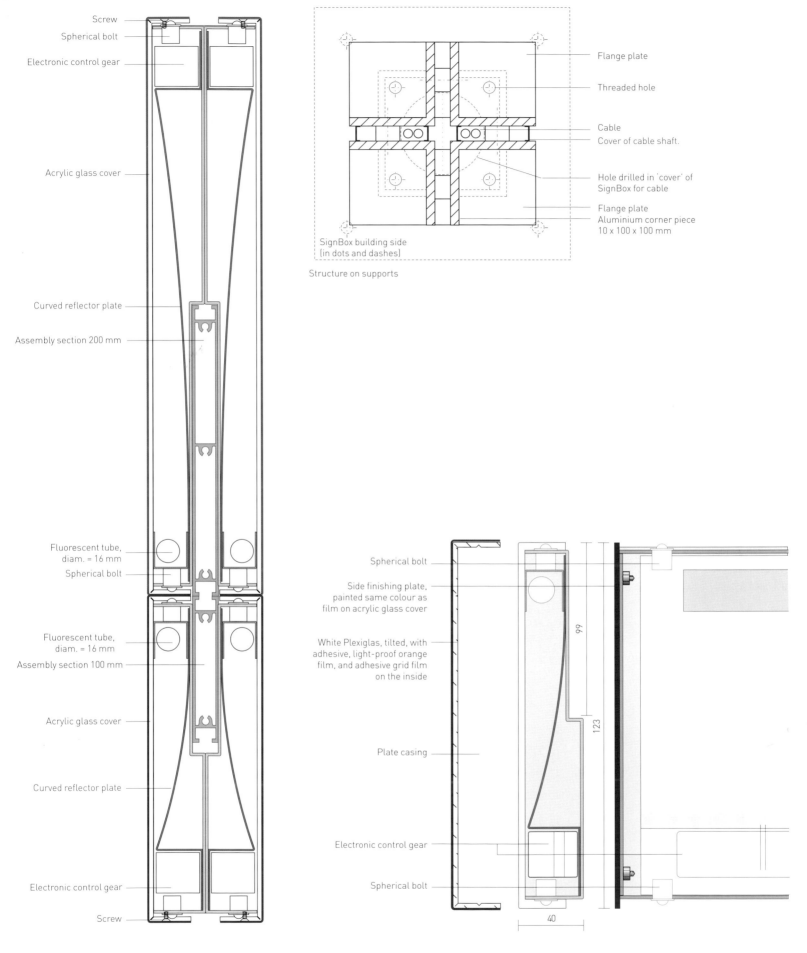

Screw

Spherical bolt

Electronic control gear

Acrylic glass cover

Curved reflector plate

Assembly section 200 mm

Fluorescent tube,
diam. = 16 mm

Spherical bolt

Fluorescent tube,
diam. = 16 mm

Assembly section 100 mm

Acrylic glass cover

Curved reflector plate

Electronic control gear

Screw

Flange plate

Threaded hole

Cable

Cover of cable shaft.

Hole drilled in 'cover' of
SignBox for cable

Flange plate
Aluminium corner piece
10 x 100 x 100 mm

SignBox building side
(in dots and dashes)

Structure on supports

Spherical bolt

Side finishing plate,
painted same colour as
film on acrylic glass cover

White Plexiglas, tilted, with
adhesive, light-proof orange
film, and adhesive grid film
on the inside

Plate casing

Electronic control gear

Spherical bolt

99

123

40

142

Airports
Cologne/Bonn Airport

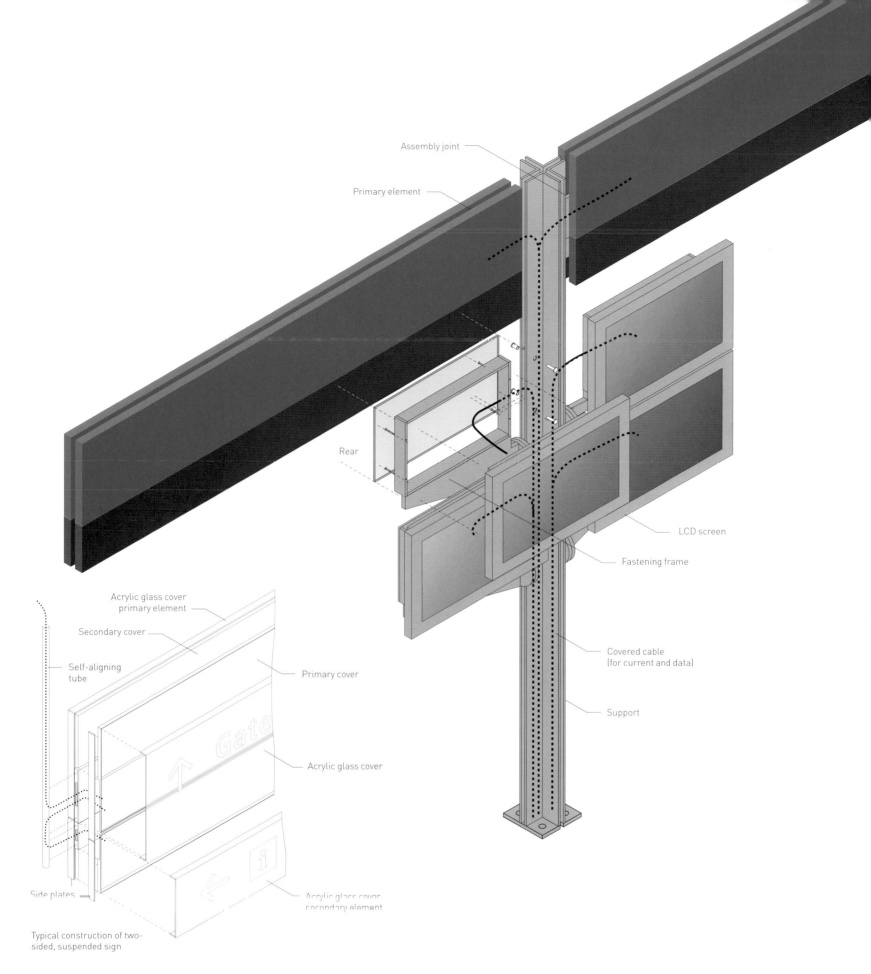

Assembly joint

Primary element

Rear

LCD screen

Fastening frame

Covered cable
(for current and data)

Support

Acrylic glass cover
primary element

Secondary cover

Self-aligning
tube

Primary cover

Acrylic glass cover

Side plates

Acrylic glass cover
secondary element

Typical construction of two-
sided, suspended sign

143

Cologne/Bonn Airport
Germany
2003
intégral ruedi baur et associés

The Cologne/Bonn Airport project was an all-embracing exercise in corporate identity which was designed to distinguish this airport from its competitors in Frankfurt am Main and Düsseldorf, and make it stand out from the uniformity of other international airports. The plan was implemented on various different levels, but focused in particular on establishing the components of the corporate identity programme both two- and three-dimensionally – superficially and spatially – so that it was felt in all sectors of the airport.

Signage is just one of these components. The various parts of the overall system together form a visual language and cannot be viewed in isolation. With regard to content and appearance, they can be reassembled to meet the requirements in different contexts. Wayfinding, for example, does not depend exclusively on familiar means such as notice boards and conventional signs, but has been designed as part of the overall layout of space, information and services in all their respective surroundings. The interplay between information and surroundings makes a major contribution to the special identity of Cologne/Bonn Airport.

Köln Bonn

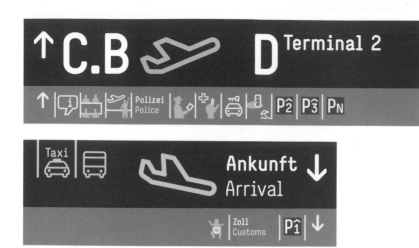

Information, top band: background, greyish blue; lettering, white; pictograms in the direction of departures and transit, blue; pictograms in the direction of arrivals and exits, green. Information, bottom band: background, orange; pictograms and lettering, yellow.

PMS 533 | PMS 1595 | PMS 572

PMS 1595 | PMS 106

The house colours are luminous and light. The mixture of these colours creates a broader and darker palette. Black and white are also used for the functional parts of the system.

Alongside typography, the pictograms are given equal status as part of the visual language of this airport. On the one hand, they can be used on signs to structure and clarify information or to identify places; on the other, they are fun. They become instruments of communication, identifying terminals, buildings, vehicles, objects and even people.

Airports
Cologne/Bonn Airport

SimpleKoelnBonn by Norm

SimpleKoelnBonn by intégral
ruedi baur et associés

The house font is inspired by the Simple typeface and developed by Atelier Norm, whose typographers were commissioned to do the redesign for Cologne/Bonn Airport. This font was chosen because it was a good starting-point for the development of a corresponding style of pictogram. The pictograms and fonts are part of the same signage family that gives the airport its identity. They are based on the same basic grid, and have a consistent degree of boldness. The fonts SimpleKoelnBonn and the symbols SimpleKoelnBonn can be used at any time in a text without causing visual disharmony. The pictograms reinforce the words, or sometimes even replace them. They can be embedded in a text, or can be made to stand out from it through colour.

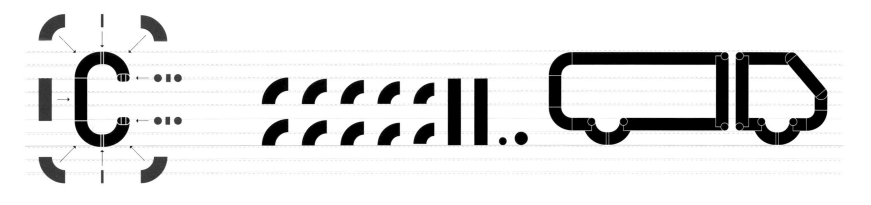

Unlike geometric pictograms, people are represented here in silhouette form. As figures, free from rigid lines, they break up the pictogram system, establishing new contexts and opening up an associative level. They convey a sense of movement and are not bound by the constraints of systematic use. These silhouettes form an integral part of the vocabulary that characterizes the airport.

Cologne/Bonn Airport has modes of signage that are far removed from conventional forms, with its open system of typography, colour, pictograms and silhouettes.

The pictorial components of the system were also adapted to bring character to functional spaces. Areas became more easily identifiable.

Inside the terminal buildings, several generations of signage systems coexist side by side, even today. The latest generation was introduced in 2000. It's rational and modular, with a contemporary structure and LED lighting. For economic reasons, it was decided to preserve the existing system, and so only the graphics and their supports were redesigned. Constructional changes and extensions were only made in those places where there were clear deficiencies in the earlier signage.

Macdonald-Cartier International Airport
Ottawa, Canada
2003
Gottschalk + Ash International, Calgary

Flying has become an increasingly stressful activity. At the Macdonald-Cartier International Airport, every effort has been made to alleviate this stress by keeping the routes between the different areas as short as possible, integrating elements such as wood and water – representing Ottawa's natural environment – and developing a wayfinding system that guides passengers in comfort. There was also a strong desire to make the airport a real gateway to Canada's capital city, and to set a standard that would impress the most seasoned world traveller.

One of the basic principles guiding the design of this system focused on the association between flying and dots of light: lights along the runways, the rows of lit windows punctuating the fuselage of a plane, the stars in the sky, the lights of the city below from the plane. This idea led to a design that revolved around chains of lights, and particularly an arrow of lights against a grid of dots. In order to fit in with the architecture of the new terminal, directional signs were set up on posts, allowing an unobscured view of the building, with all the information well above head height.

The name of the airport is written in huge letters against a background of dots on two sides of the building – facing out towards both incoming road and air traffic. These are the only signs on the outside of the building, giving a visual foretaste of the dot theme throughout.

The pictograms correspond to the North American pictogram system for traffic and transport.

The signs for the toilets display a pictogram and a text in two languages. The signage is in accordance with the American Disability Act (ADA). The letters are raised by 3 mm so that they can be recognized by touch and read as braille.

Thesis, The Mix Bold for English and Thesis, The Mix Bold Italic for French. The Canadian government stipulates that equal weight should be given to both languages.

aabbccddee

Thesis, The Mix Bold and
Thesis, The Mix Bold Italic

The dimensions of the signs are built on a 150 mm grid.

Long signs suspended from the ceiling are supported by a steel wire at the yellow tip.

Giant arrows direct
passengers to the
terminals for flights
to the USA or Canada.

Main notice boards:
double column with
two information boards
1,200 x 1,800 mm and
LED arrows.

112233

Thesis, The Mix Bold and
Thesis, The Mix Bold Italic.

PMS 138   PMS 653

Primary information: pictograms are placed above the text. Vertical height: 75 mm. Line spacing: 425 pt, c. 150 mm. The position of the text and pictograms is determined by the illuminated arrow in the yellow panel.

Pictograms of 300 and 350 mm can also be used without any text. For optical reasons, pictograms are placed 5 mm outside the boundaries of the grid.

Secondary information: the text is laid out next to the pictogram. Pictogram: 135 mm. Vertical height: 50 mm. Line spacing: 212 pt, c. 76 mm.

If there is only one item of information, the pictogram can also be placed above the text.

Additional visual signs such as flags or logos (e.g. for car rentals) are placed 50 mm from the pictograms and centred.

Primary information is laid out at the top of the sign, and secondary information below. Information of differing importance or context is separated by a yellow line 4 mm thick or, if possible, by a gap.

Gate numbers are always laid out next to one another on one line.

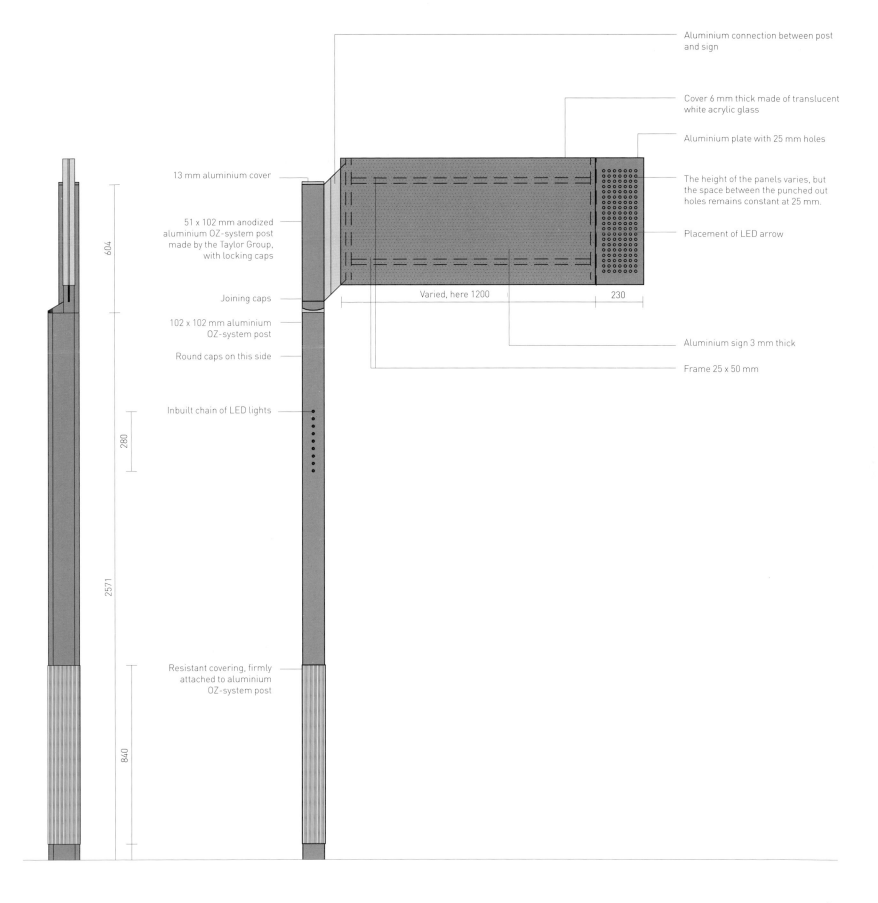

Aluminium connection between post and sign

Cover 6 mm thick made of translucent white acrylic glass

Aluminium plate with 25 mm holes

13 mm aluminium cover

The height of the panels varies, but the space between the punched out holes remains constant at 25 mm.

51 x 102 mm anodized aluminium OZ-system post made by the Taylor Group, with locking caps

Placement of LED arrow

Joining caps

102 x 102 mm aluminium OZ-system post

Round caps on this side

Varied, here 1200

230

Aluminium sign 3 mm thick

Frame 25 x 50 mm

Inbuilt chain of LED lights

Resistant covering, firmly attached to aluminium OZ-system post

604

280

2571

840

Schiphol Airport
Amsterdam, Netherlands
2003
Bureau Mijksenaar

Bureau Mijksenaar has been in charge of Schiphol Airport's signage system since 1990. In 2001, the whole system was modernized. It had become apparent that all the general and wayfinding maps (including their fastenings and supports) for guiding passengers and visitors round the airport needed attention. It was also decided that shops and restaurants would be given greater priority under the new system.

There were therefore three main objectives: to develop a new wayfinding system, including newly designed signs and supports; to incorporate more detailed information about shops and restaurants; to make the new signs as straightforward as possible, despite the additional information to be included. The solution was to provide central information points that function both as signposts and as wayfinding maps. These central points use the same graphics, colours and pictograms as the overall signage system. The design and choice of materials enhance the interior design of the terminal, but above all display clearer directions to shops and restaurants without in any way impinging on the general overview.

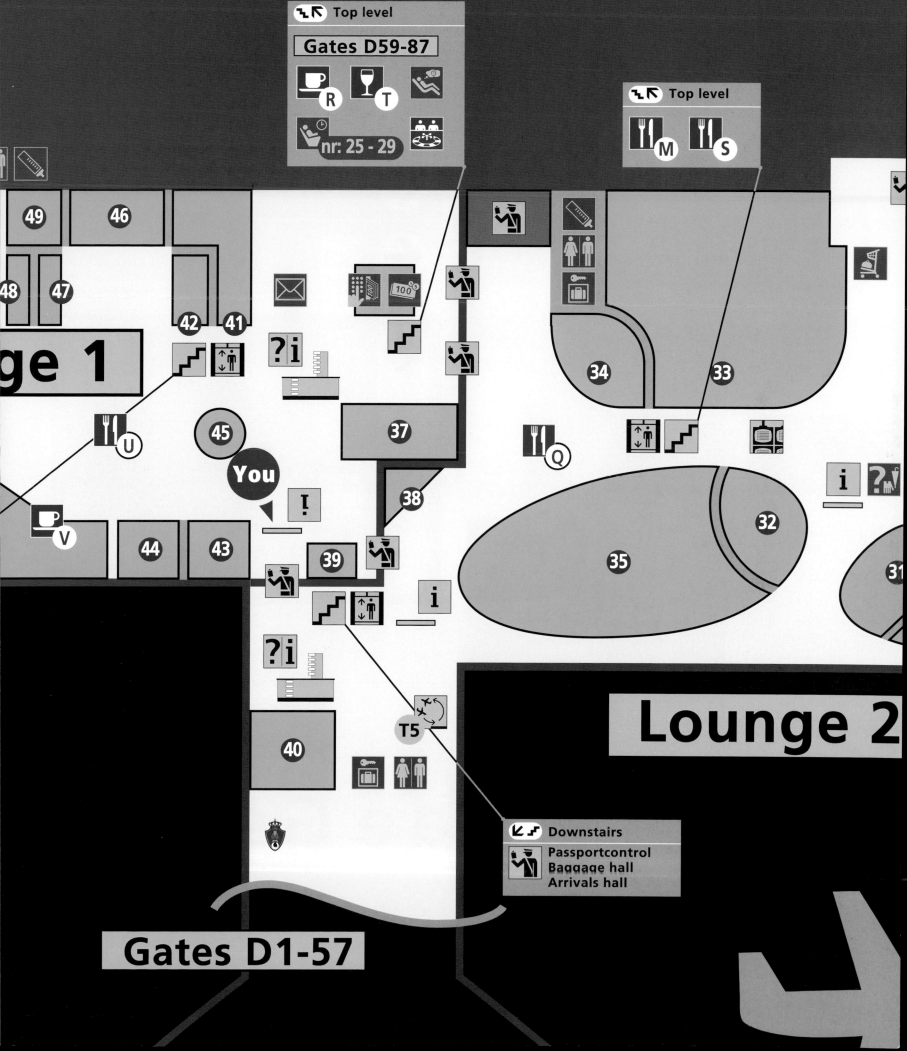

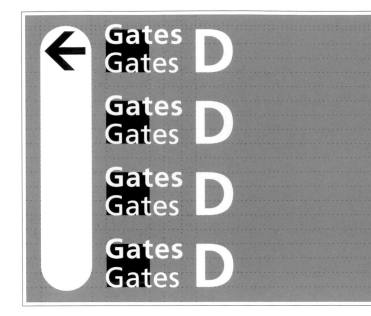

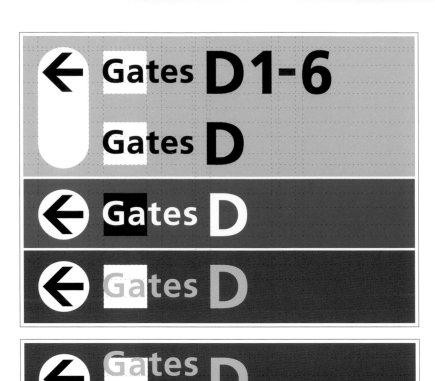

PMS 432
Waiting rooms

PMS 123
Arrivals and departures

PMS 355
Emergency exits

PMS 301
Shops and restaurants

Frutiger Bold and Roman for light text on dark background. Frutiger Schiphol Bold for dark text on light background. This is a slightly thicker version of Frutiger, in order to achieve an optimal balance between light and dark, while giving the letters the same degree of boldness.

a e G s t 16
a e G s t 16

Frutiger Bold (Outline) and Roman, Adrian Frutiger, 1976, and Frutiger Schiphol Bold

1240   1550   1860   2160   2480   3060

25
475
700
925

33,75 11,25
55
45 35
45
45

Gates **D1-6**
Gates

Gates **D**
Gates

Gates **D**
Gates

Gates **D**
Gates

45   157,5   45   135   45   45   22,5 22,5

After the fire at Düsseldorf Airport, emergency exit signs in Amsterdam were also changed. Green, which had previously been used for services, is now reserved exclusively for escape routes.

The system of emergency exits consists of large signs placed 50 m apart. Maps showing all the escape routes provide a back-up.

The central information points are framed and double-faced to maximize impact. Additional stands contain folding maps, which passengers can take away with them.

The system is designed to be user-friendly. 'You Are Here' markers on airport maps pinpoint the visitors' precise locations, as well as all important destinations.

NEUES MUSEUM

The path from uncultured youth to old master or vice versa can never have been a straightforward one. Shouldn't directions also leave a few things hidden? The artistic journey is a promenade during which one gazes, gets lost in thought, or may even retrace one's steps – not so much guided as seduced. Tomorrow the exhibition will be over, and the light, bright piece of paper will be blowing in the wind, still carrying its message: Come and see me, my child. Then it will be collected and disposed of in the correct recycling bin. All that remains is our memory of the fleeting moment.

German Museum of Hygiene
Dresden, Germany
2003
Gourdin & Müller

The architect Peter Kulka took on the redevelopment of this building in 2001, and at the end of the first phase in 2003 it was officially handed over to the German Museum of Hygiene. The simplicity of the architecture was the starting-point for the design of the wayfinding system. It had to retain respect for the place itself, which meant not impinging in any way on the striking impact of the architecture.

The design of the museum, in keeping with the style of the time, is clear and symmetrical. Clear visual axes allow intuitive wayfinding, which is reinforced by a few signs that concentrate on basic information. The ideal method was to place this information directly on the walls, thus not interrupting the flow of the architecture, and there is close interplay between the structural elements and the lettering. This predominantly typographical wayfinding system, with no framework other than the walls themselves, facilitates an individual response to every feature of the building itself.

>>

Ausstellungen ___ Exhibitions ___

Toiletten ♿ ___ WC ♿

Aufzug ___ Lift ___ Ascenseur

The layout is the same for all directional signs. Where necessary, directions are supplemented by infrastructural information. All of this is given in three languages, always in the same sequence, colour and size. Arrows are situated above the first word and after the last, and the signs are either aligned to the left or the right, depending on which way they are pointing.

>>
Direktion ___ Management ___ Direction
Verwaltung ___ Administration ___ Administration
Archiv ___ Archive ___ Archives   >>

All the lettering is in Trade Gothic. This typeface is clear and concise, and its disciplined, rounded form fits in perfectly with the sober but by no means cold architecture of the museum.

<< aTRdrv 567

Trade Gothic,
Jackson Burke, 1948

Museums and Exhibitions
German Museum of Hygiene

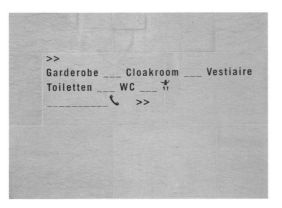

The design gives equal prominence to the three languages: German, English and French. Specially developed pictograms, light and animated in style, help to reinforce the image of the institution as a 'museum for people'.

You have arrived: here the information is like a direction without an arrow. It is always displayed centrally above the entrance, giving each place a clear identity.

PMS 186

Red was chosen for this wayfinding system. It is a clear, corporate colour, which visitors recognize immediately and can associate with the museum. It also goes particularly well with the colours of the walls (off-white, sandstone and grey tone). The lettering stands out from its surroundings, without being too overpowering.

Expo.02
Switzerland
2002
intégral ruedi baur et associés

A flexible, temporary wayfinding system devised for a specific event. Ten million visitors, four different locations, about forty exhibitions, almost all of them mounted in architectural settings specially designed for the purpose – with rail, road and water transport, and different events every day....

For the duration of the exhibition, which lasted six months, the system had to provide directions, information and identification, as well as giving prominence to the logos of the sponsors. Moreover, the system was only commissioned ten months before the grand opening. As routes and architecture had already been designed, the system had to fit in with what already existed. There was also an extremely limited budget available, which had a major influence on the visual concept of the system.

The starting-point was the creation of not just one but four visual languages. The division between cultural and infrastructural information, sponsors' logos and the Expo.02 brand led to a very simple form of support. Both the design and the graphics make the most of the temporary nature of the project: recycled objects, sometimes deliberately used in new ways, and minimal design, which makes no pretensions to aesthetic conviction, helped to create an individual, handwritten style for Expo.02.

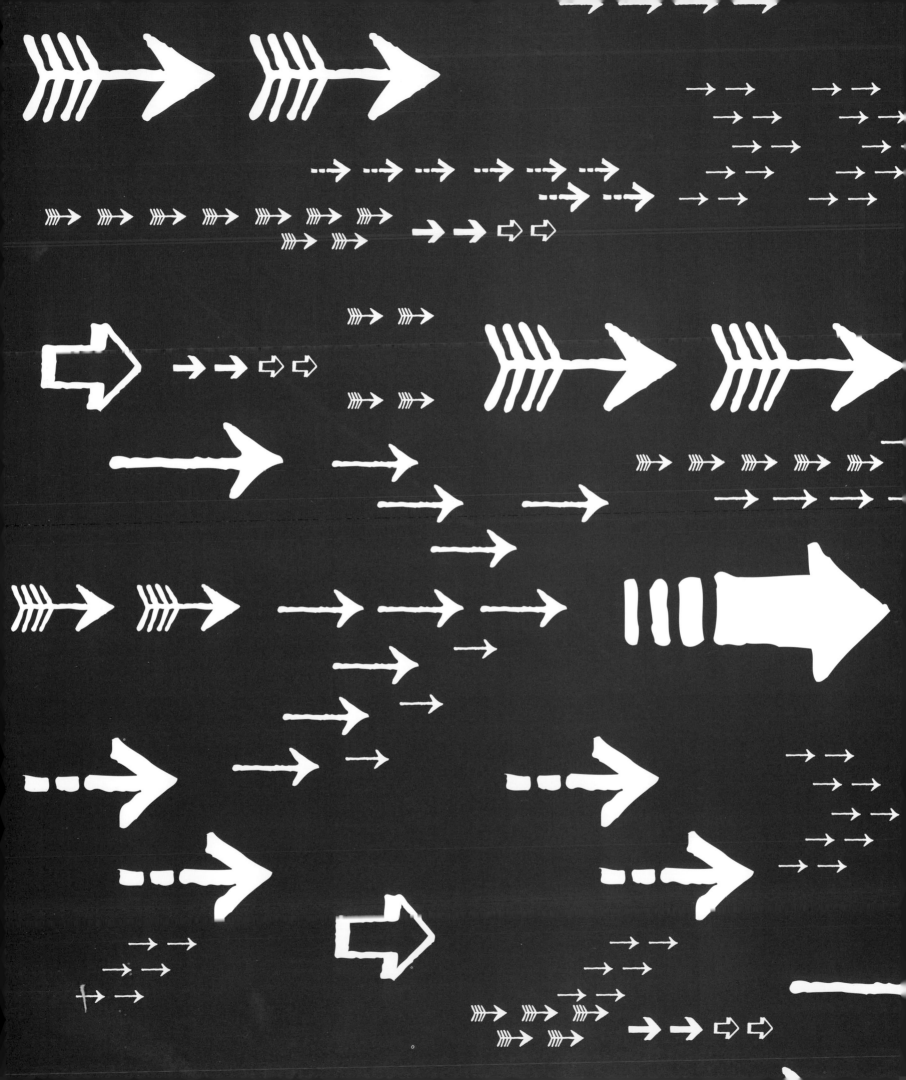

Four types of fittings were designed to distinguish between cultural and practical information, the Expo.02 brand identity and sponsors' logos.

Type A: cultural information. This was printed on light-coloured, long cloth banners, which were held in place by metal poles fixed to the ground. Additional banners were used to promote talks and other events.

Type B: service information. The wayfinding system for toilets, restaurants, meeting-places etc consisted of metal signs in conventional formats. A varied display format transformed functional information into a depiction of everyday life in Switzerland through a combination of pictograms and lettering. Lu Zhang, a Chinese artist, travelled the length and breadth of the land to observe typical features of people's daily lives.

Type C: the Expo.02 brand identity. This identified the exhibition itself. Windsocks, flags and banners, in the colours of Expo.02, were put up at all points of access to the different towns, especially at railway stations and car parks. Printed arrows on these bearers pointed the way to the 'arteplages' (temporary exhibition sites). A red balloon, visible for miles around, marked the central meeting-place at the heart of the event.

The Chinese artist Lu Zhang drew these pictograms to create a portrait of everyday life in Switzerland.

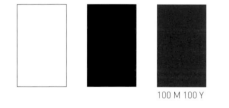

100 M 100 Y

Ak:YmR//UL**qoP

Maintax, based on
Hans Eduard Meyer's Syntax

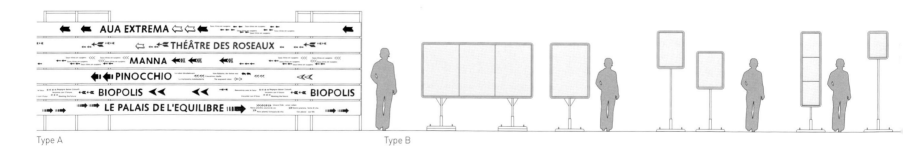

Type A

Type B

Museums and Exhibitions
Expo.02

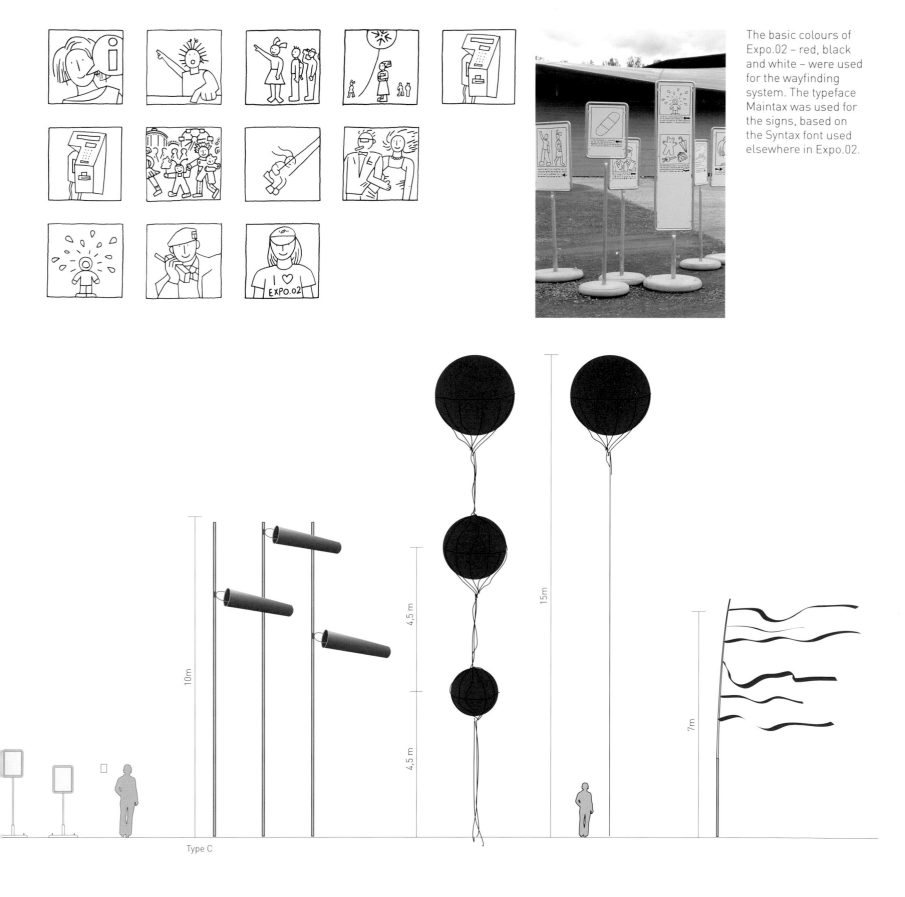

The basic colours of Expo.02 – red, black and white – were used for the wayfinding system. The typeface Maintax was used for the signs, based on the Syntax font used elsewhere in Expo.02.

Type C

10m

4,5 m

4,5 m

15m

7m

The system goes against the concept of the universal symbol. Each sign is different, depending on its context, and is accompanied by a multilingual text. The arrows are drawn by hand, in the same style as the texts and pictograms.

Museums and Exhibitions
Expo.02

Floriade Haarlemmermeer
Netherlands
2002
npk industrial design

The Dutch international horticultural exhibition Floriade took place in Haarlemmermeer in 2002. Between 6 April and 20 October 2002, three million visitors were expected for this, the biggest public event of the year. The wayfinding and information system for the 65-hectare site was designed in collaboration with the garden and landscape architect Niek Roozen. The signposts were light and simple, in keeping with the temporary nature of such events.

The system covered the whole range of signage, from simple nameplates and signposts to large-scale notice boards and general maps. Conceived for a temporary event, it used clearly defined, rectangular wooden posts with metal holders and semi-transparent plastic boards.

The signs were printed on both sides, using a fully automatic, digital colour printing process. Screenprinted colours are very robust and durable, and completely wind- and weather-resistant. The sizes of the signs varied according to their function, between 25 x 25 cm, 35 x 35 cm, 5 x 50 cm and 65 x 200 cm.

AakgS 19

Meta Plus Book,
Erik Spiekermann, 1991

aMgp345

Quadraat Italic,
Fred Smeijers, 1996

Museums and Exhibitions
Floriade Haarlemmermeer

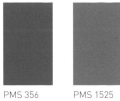
PMS 356

PMS 1525

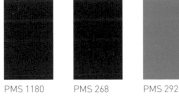
PMS 1180   PMS 268   PMS 2925

PMS 229

PMS 130

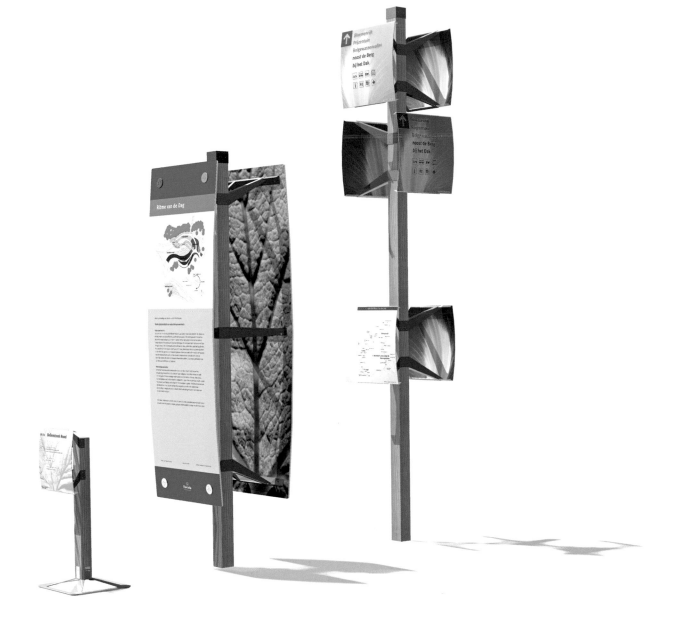

MoMA QNS
New York, USA
2002
BaseNYC

In 2001, the Museum of Modern Art temporarily moved house to Long Island City, Queens. BaseNYC was given the task of creating a visual identity for the museum. Pictograms and lively but easily identifiable graphic elements were designed to complement the features of the museum. Following the signage systems used in airports, and their common abbreviations such as LAX and JFK, the team settled on the name QNS (Queens).

ARos 67 NH8g PQs1

Franklin Gothic Roman,
Morris Fuller Benton, 1903

Office Bold and Regular,
Stephan Müller, 1999

Museums and Exhibitions
MoMA QNS

PMS 284

The rich blue colours take up those of Swingline, the stapler factory formerly housed in these premises. They fit in well with the surroundings.

Working together with the architect Michael Maltzan, BaseNYC developed a new identity for the museum, using a system of typefaces and wayfinding that was integrated directly into the architecture both inside and outside. The architecture also functioned as a platform for advertisements and announcements of exhibitions,

In order to exploit the exposed situation of the museum, information was posted on the exterior walls and on large-format banners and posters.

Museumsinsel Berlin
Germany
2004
Polyform

Museumsinsel ('Museum Island') in Berlin is an historic ensemble of museums and in 1999 was placed on UNESCO's World Heritage list. A master plan was drawn up to renovate these historic buildings and give them a contemporary infrastructure, and Polyform were commissioned to design a system embracing corporate design, wayfinding and information, new media and on-site communications.

The system will welcome visitors on the opposite bank of the river, accompany them across to the island, into the buildings (still in the process of development) and finally to the collections.

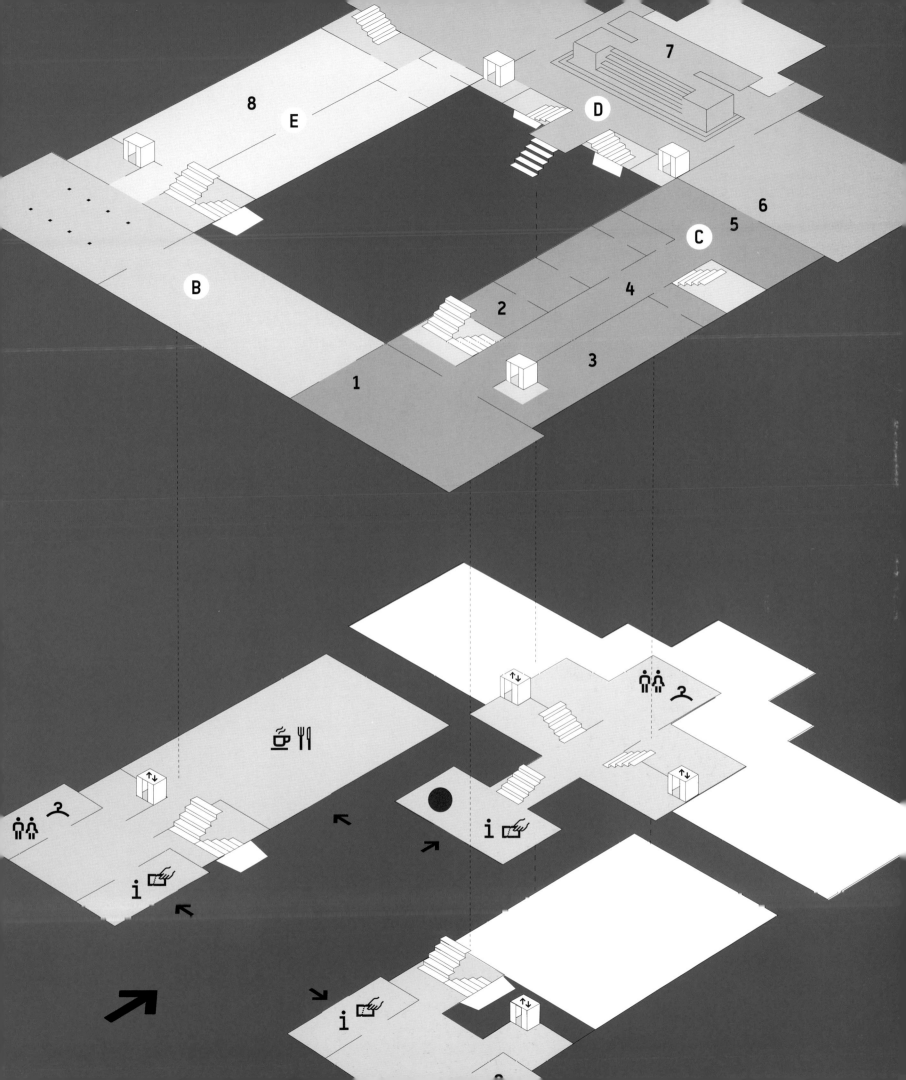

The colour scheme consists of basic and atmospheric colours. The basic colours take their tone from the buildings, rooms and objects on display, drawing on materials such as sandstone, ivory, bronze and marble, and have been selected to provide a restrained, classically timeless background. The colour leitmotiv for the island is Pompeian red.

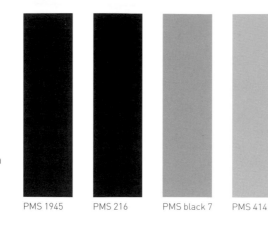

PMS 1945   PMS 216   PMS black 7   PMS 414

PMS 414 70%   PMS 414 50%   PMS 414 30%

The multifaceted nature of the museum island was the starting-point for the overall concept. Its corporate identity centres on three main areas: 'topos', 'form' and 'content', which represent the spirit and aura of this whole complex. 'Topos' stands for the ensemble in the context of the city, 'form' for the redeveloped area (architecture), and 'content' for the collections. Derived from these are the terms 'Insel' [island], 'Gebäude' [building] and 'Sammlung' [collection], which are the guiding principle and structure underlying the corporate design.

The three components of this structure function simultaneously, and are placed vertically from bottom to top. The visitor understands what is meant by the term 'museum' – which has more than one application – because the system identifies it clearly as either the building or the collection. The concepts of 'island' and 'building' continue to be signposted up to the entrance of each building, but are abandoned once the visitor is inside. Here it is the 'collection' that forms the basis of further communications. 'Highlights' lead the visitor to the main attractions.

The Museumsinsel system uses a classical serif font and a contrasting, redesigned sans serif. Sabon Next is used for the description and content of each collection, while a version of Typestar specifically modified for the island indicates buildings and other kinds of information. The words 'Museums-insel Berlin' are in MI Typestar Bold, on which the pictograms have also been based.

Pbea

Highlights,
Sabon Next Demi,
Jean François Porchez, 2002

kn ro

Collection,
Sabon Next Regular/Bold,
Jean François Porchez, 2002

Bemos

Buildings and island,
MI Typestar Bold,
Steffen Sauerteig, 1998

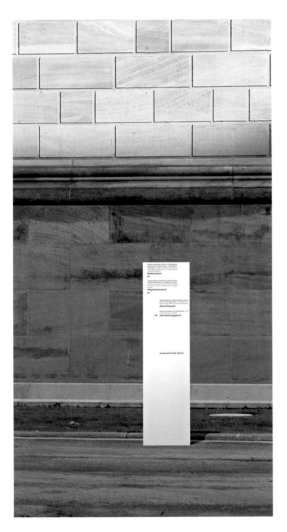

In the next few years, construction work will continue to alter the appearance of the Museumsinsel. Buildings will be closed, restored, extended and reopened. During this phase of transition, on-site communications will help visitors to find their way around the island, and will inform them about the accessibility of the collections and the progress of the master plan. 'Peepholes' are among the methods used, in addition to temporary guided tours and talks. These peepholes are small openings in the hoardings that allow visitors to watch the work in progress on the site. But only the middle one shows what is really happening. Those on the left and right offer panoramic views of the building in the past (before it was destroyed during the Second World War) and how it will be in the future after completion. They therefore offer an insight into past, present and future.

All the supports are mineral monoliths inspired by the historic stone buildings and the items in the archaeological collections. The light, almost white colour of the material ties in with one of the concepts of the corporate design: 'I am beautiful and I stand in the light.' It provides an ideal background for the coloured lettering, and these blocks distinguish themselves from the architecture without being too obtrusive or self-important. Different minerals are used, to fit in with the different temperatures and lighting conditions inside and outside the buildings, but the overall effect is one of harmony. In the areas outside, the blocks are made of high-quality, lightweight concrete. Inside, the material is artificial marble, fired several times so that it is highly resistant.

In the service areas and those not open to the public, and also in the escape routes, acrylic stone is used. From the outside areas to the interior of the buildings, the materials used for all these elements of wayfinding and information blend together to form a homogeneous whole.

National Museum of Emerging
Science and Innovation
Tokyo, Japan
2001
Hiromura Design Office Inc.

The museum is open to everyone, and it is a place where science and technology are presented as an integral part of culture. Their role in society and their possible applications in the future are also considered in a setting where ideas can be exchanged and discussed.

Symbols in the ground guide the visitors to different areas, such as the entrance, the car park, bus stops, the station, the terrace café etc.

Throughout the museum, signs are often integrated into the floor. Most are familiar to us from road signs, including warnings, directions and arrows. Although people recognize these signs, the floor is rarely used nowadays to provide information in public buildings, and it is widely assumed that signs are not very effective at floor level. Here the designers went out on a limb and risked trying something new. After all, it is a basic principle of the museum to challenge established ideas.

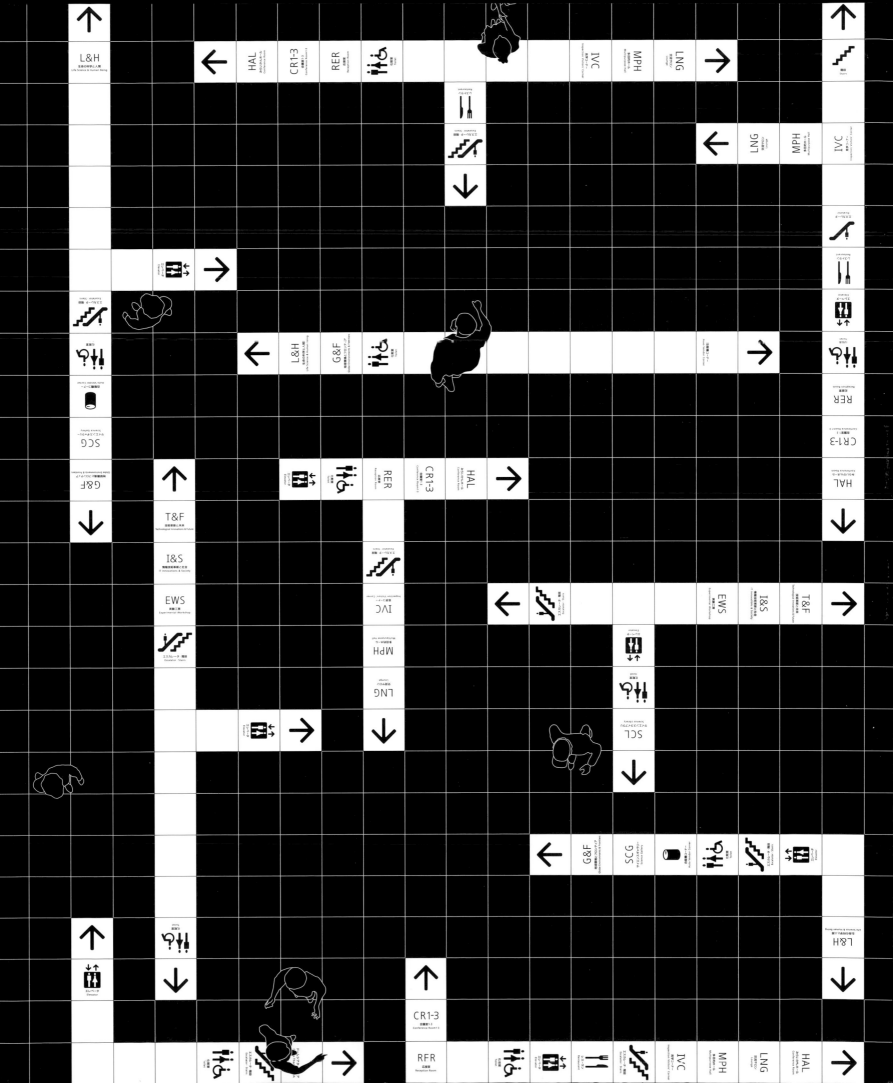

Integrating a wayfinding system into the floor of this museum was a new concept and aroused considerable opposition. The museum staff are under instructions not to hang up additional signs, but to draw visitors' attention to the fact that in this hub of future technology, the wayfinding system has every right to be innovative.

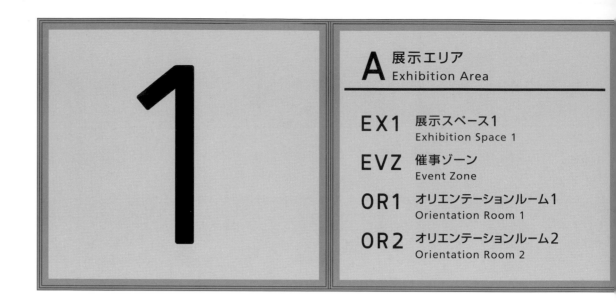

A 展示エリア
Exhibition Area

EX1 展示スペース1
Exhibition Space 1

EVZ 催事ゾーン
Event Zone

OR1 オリエンテーションルーム1
Orientation Room 1

OR2 オリエンテーションルーム2
Orientation Room 2

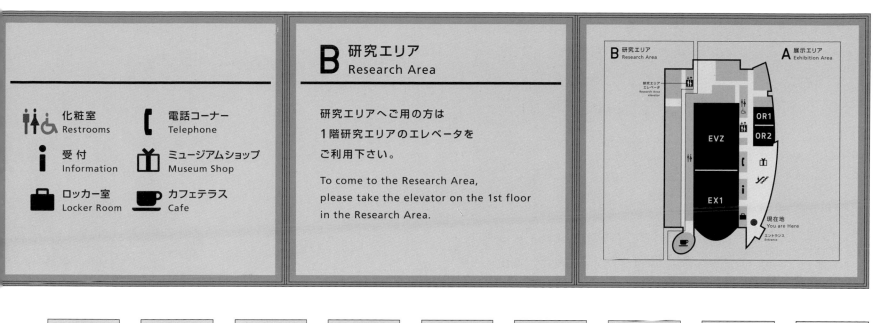

化粧室 Restrooms　電話コーナー Telephone
受付 Information　ミュージアムショップ Museum Shop
ロッカー室 Locker Room　カフェテラス Cafe

B 研究エリア
Research Area

研究エリアへご用の方は
1階研究エリアのエレベータを
ご利用下さい。

To come to the Research Area,
please take the elevator on the 1st floor
in the Research Area.

B 研究エリア Research Area　A 展示エリア Exhibition Area
研究エリア エレベータ elevator
EVZ　OR1　OR2　EX1
現在地 You are Here
エントランス Entrance

レストラン Restaurant　化粧室 Restrooms　エレベータ Elevator　エスカレータ・階段 Escalator-Stairs　階段 Stairs　電話コーナー Telephone　ミュージアムショップ Museum Shop　ロッカー室 Locker Room　自販機コーナー Vending Machine

EVZ 催事ゾーン Event Zone　SCG サイエンスギャラリー Science Gallery　GAIA ドームシアター ガイア Dome Theater GAIA　LNG 交流サロン Lounge　HAL みらいCANホール MIRAI CAN Hall　ENT エントランス Entrance　EX2 展示スペース2 Exhibition Spac　SWS 実験工 Science Workshop　SCL サイエンスライブラリ Science Library

3 — A 展示エリア Exhibition Area
EX2 展示スペース2 Exhibition Space 2
EX3 展示スペース3 Exhibition Space 3
SWS 実験工房 Science Workshop
SCL サイエンスライブラリ Science Library
化粧室 Restrooms

5 — A 展示エリア Exhibition Area
EX4 展示スペース4 Exhibition Space 4
EX5 展示スペース5 Exhibition Space 5
SCG サイエンスギャラリー Science Gallery
化粧室 Restrooms　自販機コーナー Vending Machine

6 — A 展示エリア Exhibition Area
GAIA ドームシアター ガイア Dome Theater GAIA
化粧室 Restrooms

7 — A 展示エリア Exhibition Area
HAL みらいCANホール MIRAI CAN Hall
LNG 交流サロン Lounge
INH イノベーションホール Innovation Hall
CR1 会議室1 Conference Room 1
CR2 会議室2 Conference Room 2
CR3 会議室3 Conference Room 3
化粧室 Restrooms　レストラン Restaurant

3173

600

OR1·2 — Redesigned Frutiger
オリエンテーションルーム1・2
Orientation Rooms 1-2 — Frutiger 55 Roman

500　500

CRH-3

Frutiger 55 Roman,
Adrian Frutiger, 1985

CRH-3

Redesigned version

As floor signs need to display information as succinctly as possible, rooms are identified by pictograms and letters. Upper-case letters were used for this purpose, but the existing font was not suitable. Using the Frutiger as its basis, a new font was designed to meet the requirements of the museum. It is a monospace font and, in comparison to its predecessor, has clearly rounded corners.

To stop visitors from slipping, the floor has been fitted with dot-shaped glass beads. The symbols are backlit, and the individual signs under the glass can easily be changed.

Museums and Exhibitions
National Museum of Emerging Science and Innovation

The avoidance of colour has contributed to the calming atmosphere, while the signs themselves are in harmony with the architecture and do not compete with the exhibits for attention. The wayfinding system is multilingual, as the museum attracts many visitors from abroad. The system is intended to help people find their way without forcing them to go in any particular direction.

The wayfinding system is in black and white, as both client and architect wanted an unobtrusive design.

PASS (Parc d'aventures scientifiques)
Frameries, Belgium
Since 1999
BaseBRU

BaseBRU developed the logo and image of the PASS interactive science museum on the Franco-Belgian border. The complex stands on the site of a disused colliery, and comprises the redeveloped original buildings, which are linked together by passages. The contract demanded an image and wayfinding system that would fit in with the unusual character of the buildings.

There were four stipulations relating to the wayfinding system. It had to: include four languages (French, Dutch, English and German); be smart and easily understood by children, who are the main target group; respect and reinforce the nature of the architecture; and be economical.

BaseBRU designed a signage system that gave each individual building its own colour and number. This code runs consistently throughout the system, on printed matter, screens, digital applications including the Internet, and of course all signs.

1) The footbridge PMS 116
2) The children's street PMS 158
3) The belvedere PMS 032
4) The pit-head frame PMS 204
5) The machine room PMS 2592
6) The exhibition hangar PMS 2935
7) The hall of images PMS 319
8) The silo building PMS 375
9) The containers PMS 379
10) The adventure garden PMS 574

01

02

03

04

05

06

Aaek 01

FF DIN, Albert-Jan Pool, 1995

07

08

09

10

Museums and Exhibitions
PASS

Pictograms, numbers and colours are on the walls, floors, ceilings, lift doors etc. This colour-coded signage system is seamlessly integrated into the architecture and constitutes a central element of the park's identity.

On entering a building, the visitor goes through a 'door'. On its frame are the number and colour assigned to that building. A special floor sign acts as an additional aid.

Neue Pinakothek
Munich, Germany
2003
KMS Team

The Neue Pinakothek in Munich is one of the most important museums of 19th-century art. The original building, commissioned by Ludwig I in 1853, was destroyed during the Second World War. In 1981, Alexander von Brancas officially opened the new building. The Neue Pinakothek was given a fresh image to celebrate its 150th anniversary, and its wayfinding system was redesigned at the same time: it had to be as low-cost as possible and, without being too obtrusive, give clear directions through the very complex network of rooms. The scheme works by identifying the main route and rooms discreetly but effectively at the passageways between the different halls. The colour coding distinguishes between directions for the collection itself, which are on sand-coloured signs, and the foyer and interior court, on dark blue signs.

Theresienstraße

abdHQ 150

abdHQ 150

FF DIN, Albert-Jan Pool, 1995

The font chosen for this system was FF DIN, the house font of the three Pinakotheken in the art district. The two styles used are Bold for German and Regular for English, but the two languages are given only where necessary – i.e. terms like 'information' or 'WC' are not duplicated. Information unconnected with wayfinding, like opening times and entrance fees, is set in two smaller font sizes.

The system of colours and font styles is maintained throughout. Font size: 127.3 pt, leading 131 pt, tracking -4. Font size: 50 pt, leading 60 pt, tracking -2. Font size: 36 pt, leading 43 pt, tracking -2.

PMS 466   PMS 5405

The shaft of the arrow has been shortened.

Dark blue is the house colour of the Neue Pinakothek, harking back to the symbolic colour of Romanticism, a main focus of the museum. The beige complements the sandstone that is characteristic of the building. The distribution of the two colours corresponds to function and architecture: in the exhibition area, the walls are covered with fabric, and the font colour is dark blue on a background of beige; in the foyer and other areas, the walls are sandstone, and so the signs are in dark blue with beige lettering. The signage system is in four formats, based on a combination of two different lengths and two different widths. Short signs are used in the exhibition area on doors and to mark the wheelchair route.

Long signs are used for texts in the foyer and cloakroom area. Narrow signs are for information that requires only one line. Wide signs are for information of two lines or more (German/English).

Below: Wayfinding plan for the Neue Pinakothek.

For temporary signs in the entrance hall or next to the cloakroom, there are stands of acrylic glass, and museum staff can change the information themselves. The information is written on paper the colour of sandstone (PMS 466).

The arrow sign for the tour route is separate. This individual arrow enables visitors not familiar with the museum to follow a route through an extremely complex layout of rooms – two floors, with an '8' shaped ground plan and numerous additional galleries and internal connections. The signs are made of transparent acrylic glass 4 mm thick. These signs could easily be stuck on most surfaces, but in the foyer area acrylic glass plates were screwed onto the granite blocks to hold the signs in place.

Ramps provide access for wheelchairs and prams. The relevant information is placed at knee-level to make it easier to read.

Signs identifying the pieces of art work along the same lines as the temporary signs. Acrylic glass holders contain sandstone-coloured paper, and the museum staff can update information themselves.

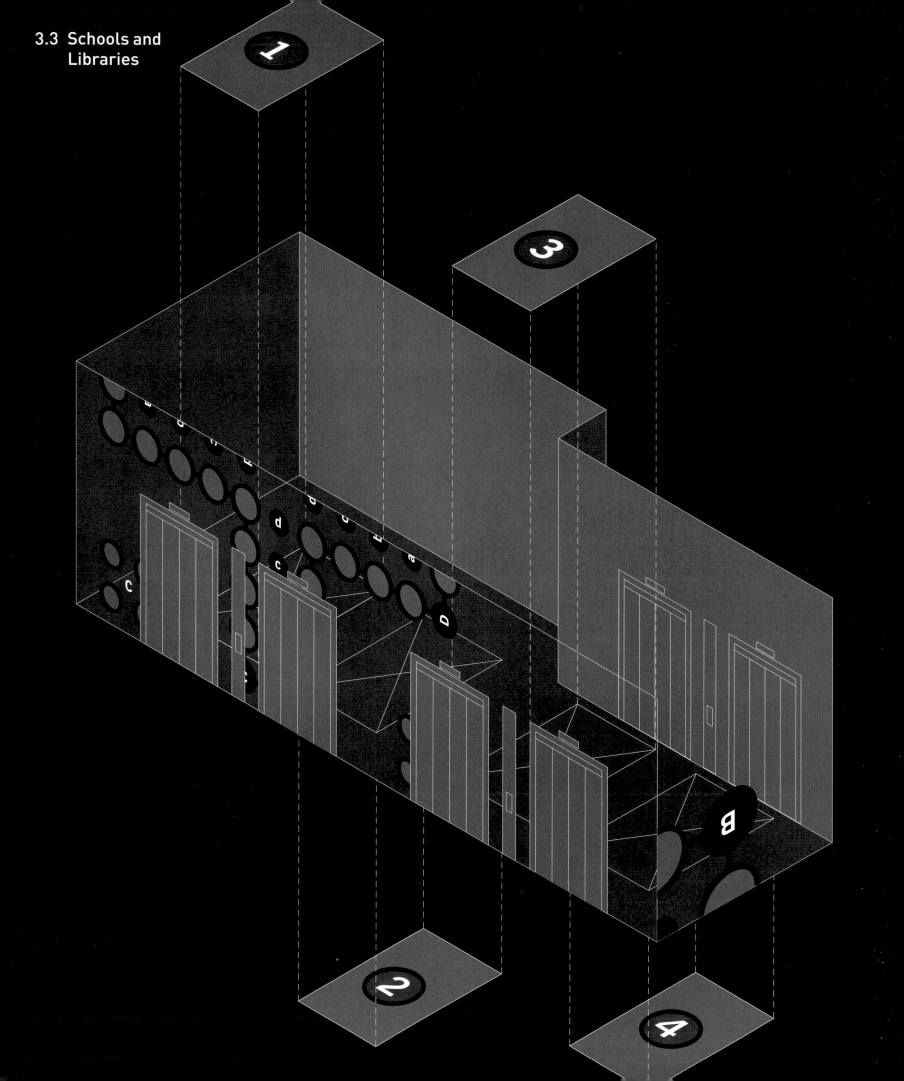

We know just how tiresome it is to decipher letters, because we've all had to learn how to do it. But deciphering these signs is fun, opening up new worlds for us. A sign may also contain a little puzzle, because without it, directions are poor and merely didactic.

Fachhochschule Osnabrück
Germany
2004
büro uebele
visuelle kommunikation

The new building for this polytechnic extends the campus to provide facilities for two faculties. The architectural design is simple: lecture halls and seminar rooms are situated along a main passage. The architects' original intention was for one of its walls to be clad with wooden slats which would contain the informational graphics. However, the initial idea to let the width of these wooden slats dictate the dimensions of the lettering did not work in practice. The light-coloured wood with the separate black bands of lettering would have looked unattractive and too obtrusive. It was therefore decided to find a single area which would fulfil all the necessary functions without impinging on the architecture. The concrete wall opposite was not suitable, as it presented a soothingly blank space that should not be broken up by graphics. There remained the ceiling – an unconventional, but for that very reason attractive idea which appealed to the client, the users and the architects themselves. The slatted wall was made of smooth plasterboard in three different shades of grey, to harmonize with the black and white wayfinding system. These subtle, barely perceptible tones enter into a dialogue with the vegetation in the courts opposite the building: bluish grey, greenish grey and reddish grey.

Above is a sky of black numbers and letters, permeated by red clouds. Like stars, the words show the traveller the path to take. The ceiling is the firmament on which the words stand, and the concrete walls remain untouched. The forward gaze of the observer naturally registers the recurring directions, which are written in letters large enough for him to grasp immediately without losing sight of the floor beneath his feet.

Aahxg
123

FF DIN Bold,
Albert-Jan Pool, 1995

Black

RAL 3018
Strawberry
red

Visitors can read the writing on the ceiling without difficulty, and without even raising their heads, because a normal field of vision can encompass the directions up to about 10 m away from the standing position. This was tested on-site with a 1:1 model. It is not possible to take in all the information from one position, and so it is repeated along the route to the respective destination.

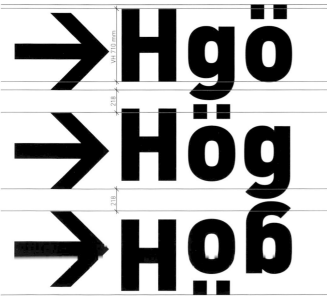

To ensure that the signs create an even pattern, line spacing was aligned with the arrows, which provide a recurrent, rhythmical feature. The descenders of the letters and the dots of the umlauts do not touch one another.

Floor levels are indicated in a soft, bluish red. The red and the black letters are the same. These red words run like a small coloured thread through a web of black and white.

The structure takes on a new dimension, as the simple austerity of the walls and floor lead up to a beautiful sky – the ceiling.

Schools and Libraries
Fachhochschule Osnabrück

The two opposite directions of the writing are laid out in such a way that they are optically balanced. During the planning stage, it was thought that one direction would be easier to read than the other from a particular standpoint, but interestingly both directions were equally readable from the same position.

Hochschule Pforzheim
Germany
2004
Braun Engels Gestaltung
(initial stage in collaboration
with Stankowski + Duschek)

The minimalist information and wayfinding system designed for the university at Pforzheim consists exclusively of signs with a matt white background. Clear, functional but lively layouts are created with typography and lines that follow a strict basic grid, and there is little or no colour. This project was first introduced in the 1990s and underwent a long period of implementation, but continues to be just as effective today as it was then. The autonomous and yet quite neutral basis of these signs allows for consistency and homogeneity throughout the new buildings on the university campus, as well as those dating from the 1970s and 1980s and the historic buildings in the centre of Pforzheim.

NCS 0080 Y
yellow for design,
NCS 0090 Y 80 R
red for technology,
NCS 1080 B
blue for economics,
NCS 3010 B 50 G
grey for administration

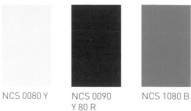

NCS 0080 Y   NCS 0090   NCS 1080 B   NCS 3010
              Y 80 R   B 50 G

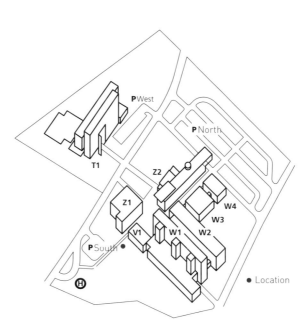

Main text
Font size: 18 mm,
measured by
H-height (= 73 pt),
leading 30 mm.
Font size of floor
levels: 33 mm VH.

Coding
Aerial plans,
alphabetical, e.g. 'T'
for the technology
building.
Main text: layout and
room numbers, purely
numerical (e.g. no
'Ground Floor' – the
levels are numbered).

Typography
Strict basic grid with
little variation in sizes
and styles, but natural
layout of information
within the grid in
accordance with
functional and
perceptual
requirements.
General and building
plans exclusively
linear, black on white,
axonometric, with
roman and bold
lettering (bold for
the area where the
observer is standing).

Sizes
Basic sign
15 cm x 15 cm:
basic dimensions
of signs (width x
height), 15 cm (door
plates), 30 cm, 45 cm,
60 cm, 90 cm, 120 cm,
180 cm, 240 cm,
300 cm; wall signs
generally have a
square format; free-
standing signs are
different heights and
widths, with the ratio
of height to width
ranging between
1:3 to 1:5.

The grid provides an
underlying, 'invisible'
basis for size, format
and layout, but it's the
surface as a whole
that determines the
structure of the
information signs,
rather than the
individual units.

Surfaces have matt white tape or powder coating, door plates paper white.

Materials and construction: cassette system of aluminium plate, edges always pre-milled and so sharp-edged, fitted flush to free-standing supports or (with wall signs) on rollback backing plates in order to create a clear gap between the sign and the wall (shadow joint, no visible fastenings).

Door signs: minimalist high-grade steel with Plexiglas sheet, paper inserts on pre-printed colour bars for laser printing according to the files supplied by the users.

Colour system only secondary and for emphasis, clearly coded: colours are assigned to individual faculties and the administration on just a few primary signs and on door plates. Here the usual black lines are replaced by colour bars.

Otherwise, the system is designed to work without any use of colour or shades of grey, thus reinforcing the scientific and analytical character of the institution.

Aaxg 123

Frutiger 67 Bold Condensed,
Adrian Frutiger, 1976.
Corporate-Design-Default

Iwadeyama Junior High School
Iwadeyama Town, Tamatsukurigun,
Miyagi, Japan
1996
Hiromura Design Office Inc.

The leitmotiv of the wayfinding system designed for Iwadeyama Junior High School is the dot.

The school has open-plan classrooms which are divided into specialist subjects, and the pupils move from one room to another according to the demands of the timetable. Movable partition walls close the rooms off from the corridor, and each room is numbered through sequences of dots punched into the sliding walls or in relief on the main walls. Boundaries between the interior and exterior of the classrooms become indistinct, giving people a new perspective on their learning environment.

The dot motif characterizes the entrance, and is continued throughout the rooms, signs, floors and lockers. The pupils adapted immediately to the open environment and the greater freedom, and lost no time in making creative use of the extra space.

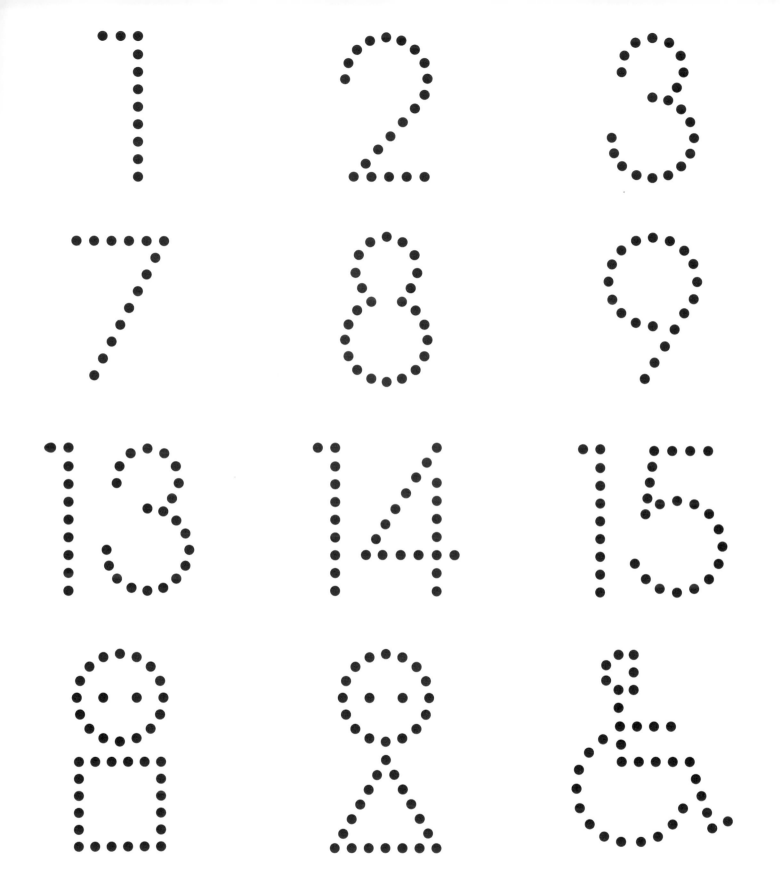

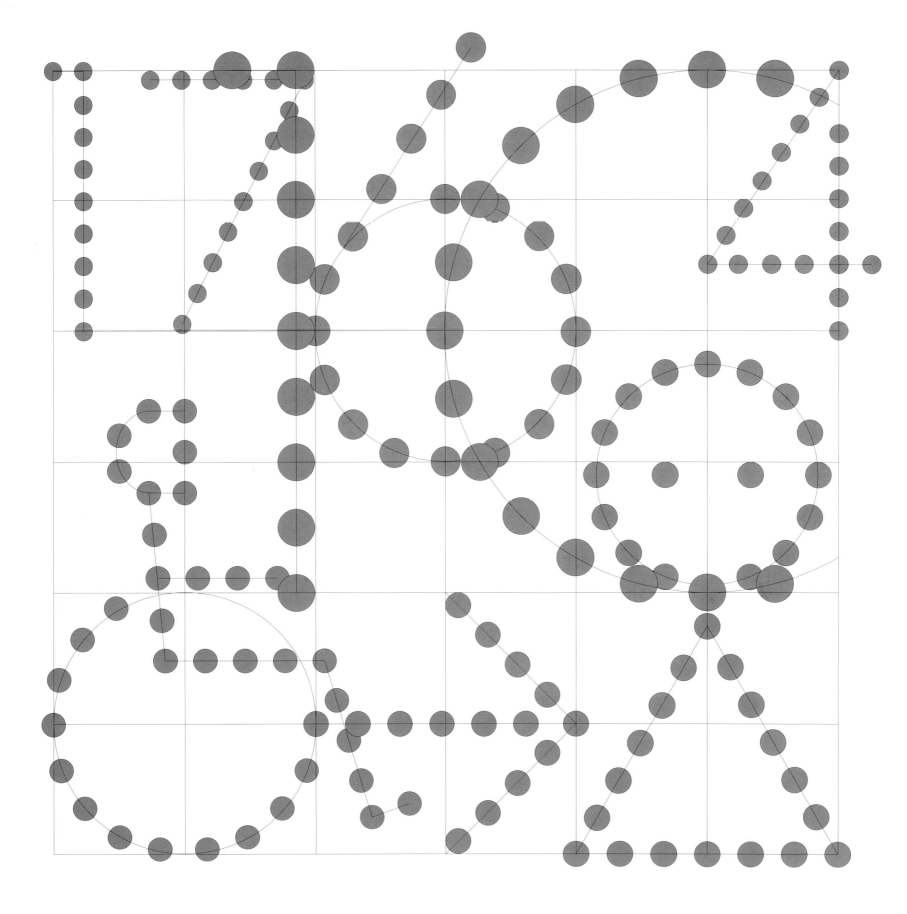

Schools and Libraries
Iwadeyama Junior High School

Lucent Technologies Center for Arts Education
Newark, USA
2001
Pentagram Design, New York

The Lucent Technologies Center for Arts Education is a relatively new school attached to the New Jersey Performing Arts Center (NJPAC) in Newark. The new building is directly adjacent to the site of the NJPAC, and is financed through a foundation established by Lucent Technologies. The stone edifice, originally constructed as a manse in the 1940s, covers an area of about 2,800 m^2 and is as sternly impressive as any old school house.

NJPAC wanted to make this somewhat grim-looking building more attractive. However, as the budget was tight, there was no question of a complete renovation. The designers were commissioned to divide the building up and use graphics to give the exterior a fresh and unmistakable identity of its own. They painted the exterior white and covered it with bright inline type, reminiscent of theatre posters. Evocative words such as 'poetry', 'music', 'drama', 'dance' and 'theater' run across the façade in a higgledy-piggledy pattern and are complemented with coloured banners, thus transforming the school into a lively symbol for this area of the city. In the interior, an explosion of colour creates a happy atmosphere, and at no great expense.

Schools and Libraries

Tiles of industrial
linoleum were laid in
diagonal, chequered,
wedge-shaped,
striped and
rectangular patterns
of red, yellow, green,
black and grey.
The radiators and
fireplaces are in
the same colours.

Schools and Libraries
Lucent Technologies Center for Arts Education

A fine example of how a building can be transformed by an expert use of lettering. It imparts a cheerful tone to the urban setting, giving the place a unique identity that could not have been achieved by the architecture alone.

Cafeteria, Stuttgart University
Germany
2004
büro uebele
visuelle kommunikation

The university cafeteria in Stuttgart-Vaihingen is a special place. This poetic space was designed with Swiss precision by Atelier 5 in 1970, and carefully renovated by the same firm thirty years later. The architects decided to bring in a graphic designer for the handful of signs. The task was simple: thirteen places needed to be marked and clearly visible from different perspectives. The ground plan was studied, and the best locations identified in relation to the entrances and the target area. The information had to be positioned very high up, so that it could be seen above the heads of the people milling around in the foyer during the busiest times. From the points marked on the ground plan the system started to take shape, consisting of long tubes extending from the floor to the ceiling.

The foyer is an area of flow – a concrete sculpture in the middle of a concrete structure. Both inside and outside, the route is marked with fluorescent red tubes, up to 6 m high. Their smooth, round forms seem to break free from the orthogonal grey concrete that surrounds them. Through their shape and artificial colour they are able to stand out from the architectural setting, but these distinguishing features also make them more readable.

Aag
hx
123

Avenir 85 Heavy,
Adrian Frutiger, 1988

The lettering is clear, soft and rounded, like the tubes themselves. The colour (RAL 3024 luminous red) stands out very effectively from its concrete, grey surroundings. It is very much a colour of our time, linking up with the existing brightness inherited from the 1970s.

Schools and Libraries
Cafeteria, Stuttgart University

The diameter of these seamless tubes, which are anything up to 6 m high, strikes a good middle ground: it is too big for them to be mistaken for gas or drainage pipes, but too small for them to be seen as supports. By setting the lettering diagonally across the curved surface, the type can be larger than if it were strictly vertical. Had the type run vertically, the ascenders and descenders would have made it more difficult to read. As they are, the eye can fill in the blanks. The oblique lettering also looks better.

225

Parsevalschule Bitterfeld
Germany
2000
büro uebele
visuelle kommunikation

The design for this vocational school took its lead from the architecture. The U-shaped ground plan with several entrances required an information system that would offer visitors and pupils a clearly prioritized set of directions. The hierarchy was set up typographically: the visitor's location was given the largest type size; those parts of the building that were further away were given smaller letters; and the smallest font was reserved for the infrastructure (e.g. gymnasium, secretary's office). Visually, this distinction seems almost exaggerated. The large signs on the walls, laid out on a grid, play with the available surfaces, while the rhythm of the lettering responds to the surrounding space.

Who are these large wall signs aimed at? On the first day of term, hundreds of new pupils will be searching for their classrooms or labs. The building will be filled with a medley of different colours, noises and smells, not to mention things flying through the air. The huge signs on the walls offer a helping hand to lost pupils, with their clear though never intrusive directions.

This wayfinding system stands tall amid the swirling flood of newcomers. It also meets the needs of both client and architect, who wanted a precisely formulated syntax of signs and pictograms, levels and sections to complement the plain and simple language of the building – a system that provided both wayfinding and typographical adornment. The result was a signage system that adapted itself naturally to the architecture, communicated the necessary information, but resisted putting aesthetics before efficiency.

The grid allows a flexible approach to different architectural contexts. On the large surfaces of exposed concrete, the graphics have a great deal more freedom. If the space is restricted, or there is a fire alarm in the way, the lettering can skirt around it, and the composition can be tightened without seeming disorganized.

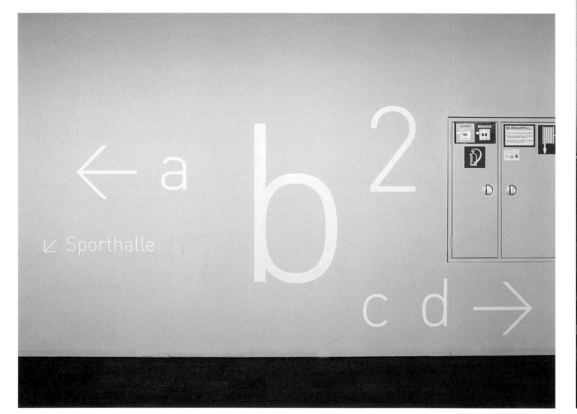

Albert-Jan Pool's FF DIN was designed in 1995. It is a beautiful, functional font, which fits in well with the clear and simple nature of the architecture.

abc D 023
abc D 023

FF DIN Light and Medium,
Albert-Jan Pool, 1995

Schools and Libraries
Parsevalschule Bitterfeld

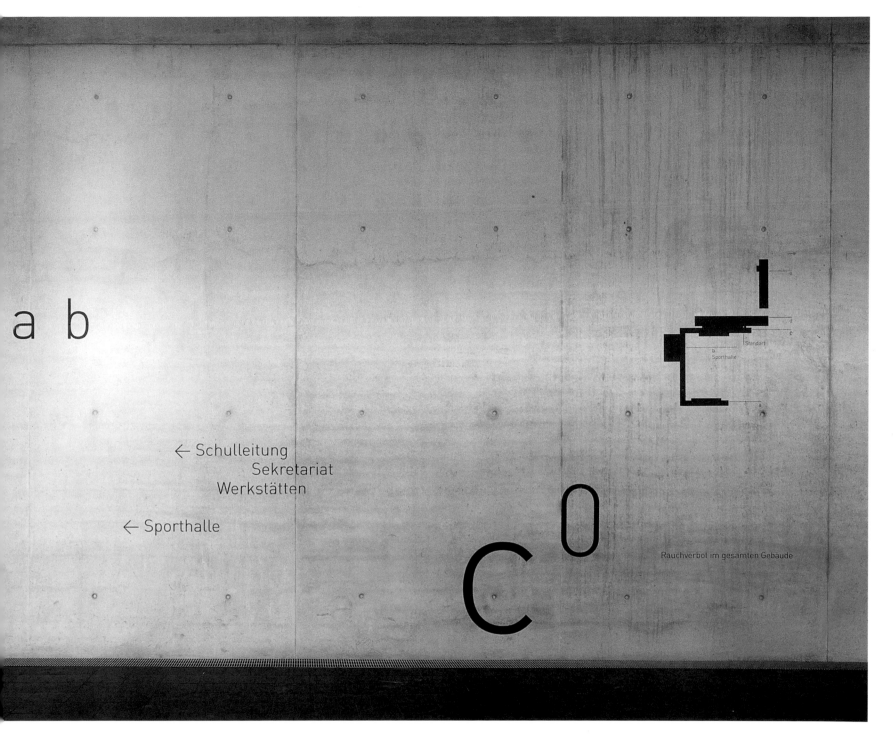

a b

← Schulleitung
Sekretariat
Werkstätten

← Sporthalle

C⁰

Rauchverbot im gesamten Gebäude

On exposed concrete,
the signs and lettering
are in anthracite
grey, but on coloured
surfaces they are silver.

One big advantage
of FF DIN is its arrows,
which go with any style
of font.

C²

Werkstätten

Sporthalle →

→

The client wanted a bust of Parseval, the man from whom the school takes its name. This kind of request can turn into an embarrassment if the quality is not up to scratch. Here, a portrait of Parseval was integrated into the architecture. The image is made up of many squares of different sizes on translucent sandblast-effect film.

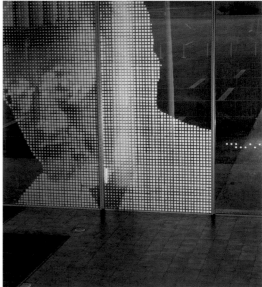

Schools and Libraries
Parsevalschule Bitterfeld

Lettering, arrows and general plans are organized on a grid that governs the hierarchy of the information. The largest sign indicates where you are standing at that point; the next size down identifies areas nearby. The horizontal spacing between the different sizes is fixed, corresponding to a particular number of units on the grid.

The grid unfolds vertically using the smallest font size (which denotes those sections of the building that are furthest away) as its starting-point. See also page 41.

Saitama Prefectural University
Koshigaya City, Saitama, Japan
1999
Hiromura Design Office Inc.

On the huge campus of Saitama Prefectural University stand the 200-m long buildings of the university and the Junior College opposite. In the court between the main buildings are facilities used by students from both institutions. The grassy roofs of these secondary buildings provide terrace-style crossings between the main buildings, and scattered haphazardly around the court are laboratories, a library and seminar rooms. It's like a labyrinth – as soon as you enter it, you are lost. For this reason, figures were designed and placed where they could be seen from every position in the maze.

The figures, which seem to stretch out a hand, are made of black metal plate. They combine the functions of sign and artwork.

All the plans are drawn from the perspective of the observer. Visitors are easily able to pinpoint where they are, and can then work out the direction and distance between them and their destination. The signposts follow the same principle. The formal language of the graphics is consistent and blends in with the rest of the wayfinding system.

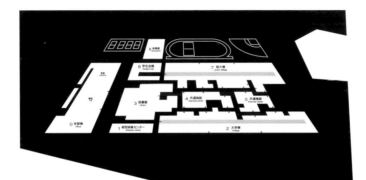

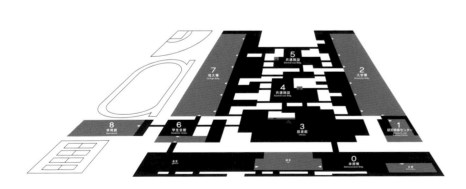

Schools and Libraries
Saitama Prefectural University

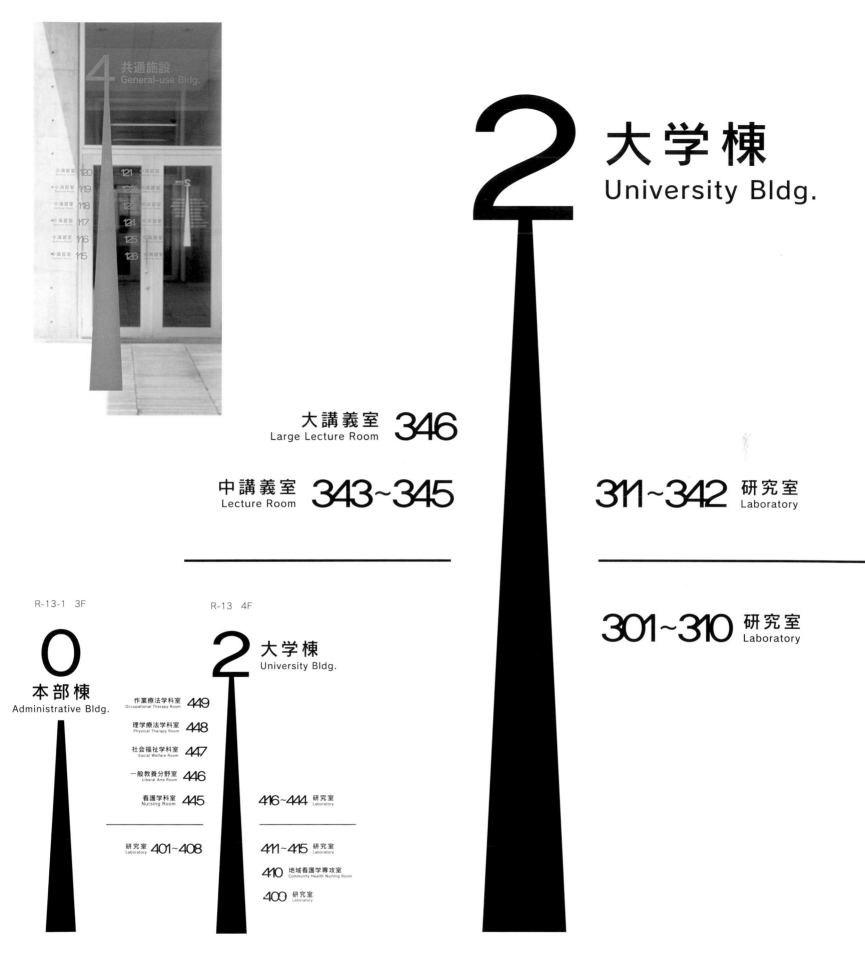

4 共通施設
General-use Bldg.

小演習室 120 121 小演習室
小演習室 119 122 中演習室
小演習室 118 123 中演習室
小演習室 117 124 中演習室
小演習室 116 125 中演習室
小演習室 115 126 小演習室

2 大学棟
University Bldg.

大講義室 346
Large Lecture Room

中講義室 343~345
Lecture Room

311~342 研究室
Laboratory

301~310 研究室
Laboratory

R-13-1 3F

0 本部棟
Administrative Bldg.

R-13 4F

2 大学棟
University Bldg.

作業療法学科室 449
Occupational Therapy Room

理学療法学科室 448
Physical Therapy Room

社会福祉学科室 447
Social Welfare Room

一般教養分野室 446
Liberal Arts Room

看護学科室 445
Nursing Room

416~444 研究室
Laboratory

研究室 401~408
Laboratory

411~415 研究室
Laboratory

410 地域看護学専攻室
Community Health Nursing Room

400 研究室
Laboratory

The two 200-m long main buildings, which stand opposite each other, are made of prefabricated concrete blocks. From the different crossings it is difficult to distinguish a particular room with the naked eye, and so large numbers have been suspended from the ceiling to identify each location.

These numbers contain three digits: the first denotes the floor level, and the other two indicate the room. As it proved to be technically impossible to hang the three digits separately, they had to appear as a single number. They therefore all had to be the same height – so rounded digits that would normally fall below the baseline, such as 3, 5, 6, 8 and 0, had to be exactly the same size as the rest. These same digits were also used on the bookshelves and in the reading-rooms throughout the library. The polished, high-grade steel shelves reflect the books opposite, giving them an almost insubstantial appearance. White numbers seem to hover over the books, and help to create an unusual feeling of space.

Seattle Public Library
USA
2004
Bruce Mau Design

The new Seattle Public Library – covering an area of 33,000 m² – was designed by the Office for Metropolitan Architecture (OMA) under the direction of Rem Koolhaas, and was opened in 2004. This striking building is a central feature of Seattle's cultural and communal life. In addition to the vast number of books, the library houses official publications, periodicals, audiovisual materials, and the technical facilities to gain access (also online) to the current catalogue. Each day, between 6,000 and 8,000 visitors use the library to take advantage of all that the city has to offer, publically, culturally and scientifically.

The designers worked together with the architects to develop an identity, signage and wayfinding system for the building. They began by analysing ways of integrating electronic technology, bearing in mind that the library is a public institution that helps to create a community and offers an open forum for discussion and debate.

The basic concept underlying the signage system is a balance between the signs themselves and the architecture, with materials and dimensions made to fit in with their surroundings. Unconventional elements, such as playful, oversized 'supergraphics' and gigantic lettering on the inner and outer walls, echo the unique structure of the building.

They also cater for the needs of library users young and old. For example, the children's corner (covering an area of 60 m²) is separated from the main library by a sandblasted glass wall 4.30 m wide. Large, sandblasted signs facing towards the city can be seen from miles around.

Aahxg 123

Futura Bold,
Paul Renner, 1928

Schools and Libraries
Seattle Public Library

A characteristic feature of the library's identity is the 'Big Strong Font Made Friendly' – a font (Futura Bold) whose excellent readability makes it instantly recognizable.

The most important department is the so-called 'book spiral' for non-fiction, which is a ramp that goes right through the building on several floors. This image and the overall homogeneity of the graphics continue in the 'stack mats', which the designers made out of punched rubber.

These lie flat on the floor, but can easily be removed and laid elsewhere, so that any extension or transfer of collections can be accomplished without any fuss or extra expense.

Come rain or shine, graffiti artists shimmy up signposts and make their mark. Summer arrives and brings out the sun, which is a welcome sight for the man strolling down the street, but leaves the red paint blistering in the heat.... Of course, if this were all you thought about, you'd never design anything! A sign in a town can be like a stone flower, beautiful but never fading.

Castles, Stately Homes and
Historic Houses in Rheinland-Pfalz
Germany
2003–8
Adler & Schmidt Kommunikations-Design
with Meuser Architekten, BDA

The task was to provide tourists visiting the federal state (*land*) of Rheinland-Pfalz with a unified system of information and wayfinding throughout the castles, stately homes and historic houses. An EU-wide competition was held, inviting designs that would encompass around seventy-five historic sites in the region. A decisive factor for the judges was the idea that conventional signs which interfered with the architecture should be replaced with a mixture of different forms of communication. The place and the architecture, stripped of their directional commands, should speak for themselves and be restored to their original character.

The design eventually went back to traditional materials such as textiles, stone and bronze, and old forms of signage such as flags, banners and wall inscriptions. The information package was completed by modern multimedia and interactive technology, including digital radio and touchscreen terminals.

The different points of communication are divided initially into three different functions: starting-point, direction, destination. At starting-points like bus stops, driveways, car parks and entrances, the signs are clearly visible from a distance. Wayfinding signs are posted wherever the route may lead in more than one direction. Destination points denote all the places that have been signposted on the way.

These are then divided up again according to whether they relate to the house or history, to services, or to areas not open to the public. Signs on the site itself are limited to services such as WCs or restaurants. Places of particular historic interest can be found with the aid of a folding map or through discreet signs.

Wayfinding Map
At the heart of the system is a folding map in several languages, which serves as an entrance ticket and contains a plan of the site as well as the most important information about services.

Armed with this map, the visitor starts off on his tour of discovery, during the course of which the descriptions and explanations will enable him to identify the buildings and their historical significance.

Flags and Banners
Swallow-tailed gonfalons pinpoint the locations of the ancient monuments over long distances. There are also large flags at the various starting-points.

Textile banners, digitally printed and easy to update, display information about services at entrances, ticket-offices and administrative buildings. Steel bars and flagpoles make it easy for them to be changed.

Public Spaces
Castles, Stately Homes and Historic Houses in Rheinland-Pfalz

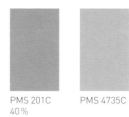

PMS 201C
40 %

PMS 4735C

Black for printed
texts, red as the
background colour
for flags, banners
and printed texts,
orange for services,
pink for English texts
and antique pink for
French.

PMS 201C,
RAL 3003

PMS 1505C,
RAL 2009

The pictograms are
line drawings, which
leave the background
intact and visible.

The special requirements of each site were ascertained on the spot with the aid of a matrix, and then a suitable solution was chosen from the list of suggestions. The graphic elements of lettering, colour and pictogram provide the visual base for the various information media, and they also create an image that is both flexible and consistent. Although the initial design and planning were expensive, this was offset by the low cost of manufacture, assembly and maintenance. The result is a modular system that preserves the character of each individual site, and at the same time meets the requirement for an information and wayfinding system that can be applied throughout the federal state, is economical and also sustainable.

These wayfinding blocks are situated at central points along the route and were created with visually impaired visitors in mind. They provide a visual and tactile aid to wayfinding around these sometimes very complex sites by reproducing the buildings and their surroundings in three-dimensional form, and information is also in braille.

The stylized models of cast bronze are mounted on concrete plinths, and in form and function represent a modern version of the old milestones.

The historical names of places and buildings are displayed in cut-out bronze letters on the walls. They are not always immediately visible, however, as their size and colour can make it difficult to distinguish them from the surface of the wall.

Nor do they make any attempt to stay true to the historic setting. The typography has been deliberately chosen for its contemporary neutrality.

The services pictograms (see page 245) play an important role in the wayfinding system. These signs, as well as short texts, can be printed with transfer tape directly onto roughcast walls, or – if the surface is not suitable for this type of printing – three-dimensional steel versions can be attached to the stone.

eaPQ567

Fago Medium, Bold
and Regular,
Ole Schäfer, 2000

In subterranean and other poorly lit areas, historical names are shown by projected lights.

So long as the situation allows it, the wayfinding system should ensure that it does not create obstacles. In order to provide information for people who are blind or visually impaired, plastic tactile signs have been mounted with a relief map, braille and large lettering.

At the castle in Ehrenbreitstein, there is a plan to lay down ground markers whose contrasting colours and materials will enable partially sighted people to find individual service points on their own.

Diemerpark IJburg
Amsterdam, Netherlands
2004
Total Identity

In 1996, Amsterdam city council decided to build the new IJburg development near the Diemerzeedijk. Until the 1930s, the proposed site had been marshland, and between 1960 and 1980 it was used as the municipal rubbish dump. As a result, it had become heavily polluted. In 1998, the site was cleared and work began on transforming it into a park and leisure centre, at the same time restoring the balance of the ecosystem. When the area had been marshland, it had supported no fewer than 236 species of birds, foxes, bats, ermine, the rare grass snake and more than 200 different kinds of plants. Once nature had recovered from the contamination, it was important to keep the leisure areas and the nature reserves completely separate.

The designers developed a signage and information system that fitted in perfectly with the character of the area, and at the same time made visitors aware that they were in a very special environment where they had to abide by the rules.

Dick Hilleniuspad

Han Rensebrinkpad

Sportpark
Inrichting na 2008

Jan Beijerpad

Diemerzeedijk

Theater

Strandje

Speelweide

Diemerpark

Diemen

Amsterdam-Rijnkanaal

Wandelroute

Zuiderzeeroute • • •

ZUIDERZEEPAD

Different types of sign have been erected to provide information and directions. There are three sorts: for information, wayfinding and prohibition. On the information pylons are facts about the history and ecology of the park, the continuing redevelopment, and the restrictions on its use. The wayfinding pylons are generally at intersections, and direct visitors to picturesque areas and those sections with particular functions. As well as showing the way, they indicate which activities take place where. Prohibition signs are situated wherever certain activities are either forbidden or restricted.

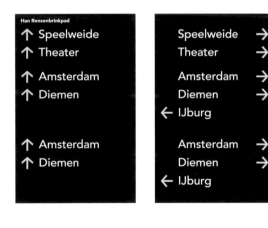

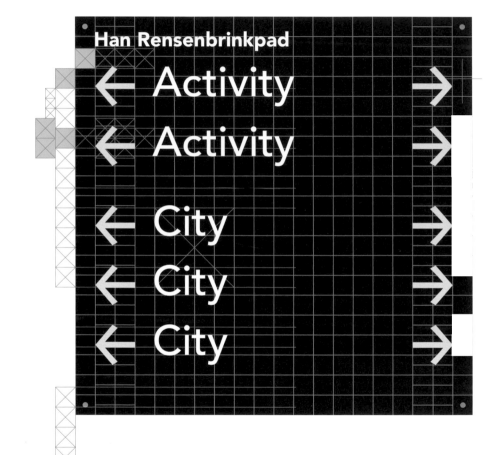

PMS 2756   PMS 2727

Hafg 45

Avenir 65 Medium,
Adrian Frutiger, 1988

The information pylons are literally landmarks, drawing attention to the entrances to the park. They are 1.8 m high, and the text is at eye level for easy reading.

The wayfinding pylons are considerably smaller, so that they cut into the surroundings as little as possible. They are 60 cm high, but are equally accessible to pedestrians, cyclists and inline skaters.

Prohibition signs apply to anyone who enters an area with designated restrictions.

Diemerpark is a well-known leisure area and nature reserve. Its redevelopment, however, is not yet complete. The renewal process is echoed by the use of colours, with a progression from black (pollution) through blue (water, air) to white (purity and cleanliness), in keeping with the process of depollution.

Avenir 65 Medium was the selected font, and Avenir is also the official font used by the city of Amsterdam. It is sans serif, very readable and ideally suited to signage.

The shape of the pylons means that information can be posted on more than one side. They are made of concrete, and the addition of black powdered lead gives them a dark hue. In time, the weather will cause the colours to fade, thus reflecting the changing nature of the land itself. The aluminium signs are centred on the pylons.

The diagrams are UV-resistant and will maintain their luminosity over a long period of time, while the signs are protected by a matt resin-based paint from which graffiti can easily be removed.

Lower Manhattan
New York, USA
Since 1996
Pentagram Design, New York

The Alliance for Downtown New York as a Business Improvement District (BID) is an association of landowners and business people whose aim is to regenerate the inner-city quarter of Lower Manhattan by attracting new businesses and residents. As well as introducing new development plans and transforming empty offices into affordable flats and retail units, they have gone to great lengths to improve the aesthetic appearance and accessibility of the local street scene.

This downtown BID embraces a network of streets covering around 12 miles, with 147 intersections. It all lies within the area south of City Hall (excluding Battery Park City, South Street Seaport and a few blocks of flats). This particular area of Manhattan is not based on the municipal grid system that makes it so easy to find one's way around the uptown streets, with their numbers and the appendage 'East' or 'West'. In downtown Manhattan, the streets do not cross one another at right angles, and they bear conventional names. The challenge, then, was to devise a way of guiding people through this inner-city labyrinth.

The signage system was originally set up in 2000. After 9/11, the signs that were destroyed on that day were replaced to fit in with the new directions for pedestrians and traffic.

PMS 485

PMS warm
grey 6

PMS 286   PMS 116   PMS 355   PMS 154

WnYhe 789

Interstate Gothic Bold
Condensed

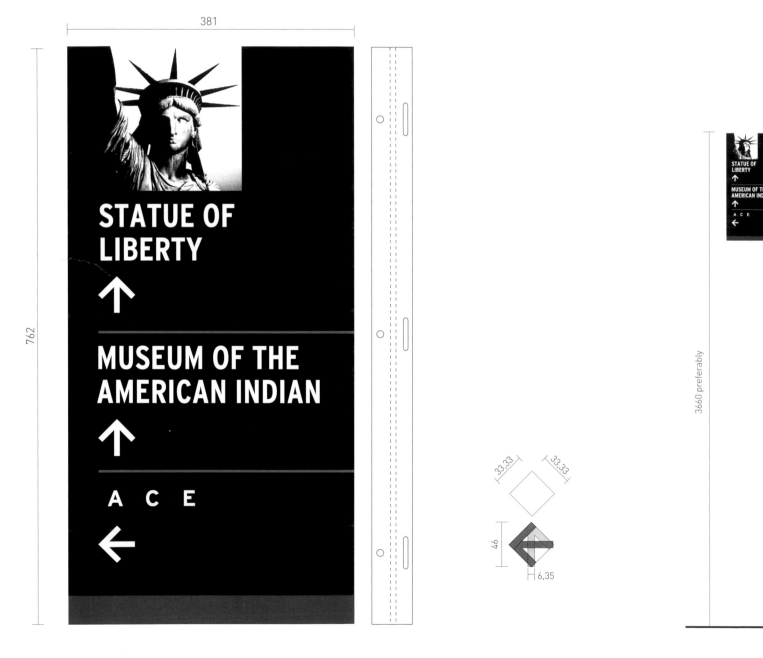

381

762

STATUE OF
LIBERTY
↑

MUSEUM OF THE
AMERICAN INDIAN
↑

A C E
←

33,33   33,33

46

6,35

3660 preferably

Public Spaces
Lower Manhattan

Digital print on double-faced aluminium plate. Directions with black-and-white grained pictures. The colours of the subway system correspond to MTA (Metropolitan Transportation Authority) defaults . The signs have been fixed to the city's streetlights, but existing traffic signs had to be left *in situ*.

Main signs: wayfinding pillars; secondary signs 1, attached to streetlights; secondary signs 2, street signs. There are also street maps of the whole district.

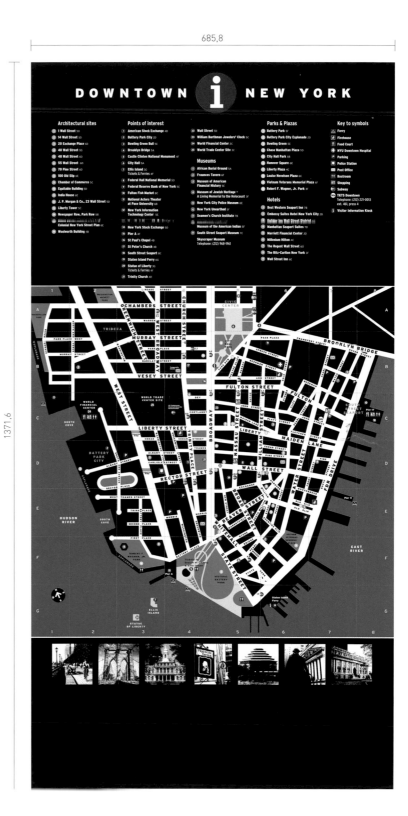

Signs showing street names and directions have been redesigned and placed in new positions, so that drivers and pedestrians can find their way more easily, and also to create a more harmonious visual effect. The result is a clear improvement, creating greater awareness of the geography of the district and the key points of interest.

The street maps and signs highlighting world-famous sights and architectural gems also improve wayfinding no end: the Statue of Liberty, South Street Seaport, Ground Zero etc. The pictures offer an extra dimension and are an effective means of overcoming language barriers.

Public Spaces
Lower Manhattan

Märkisches Viertel
Berlin, Germany
2004
Moniteurs Gesellschaft für Kommunikationsdesign
GmbH (communications design)
Griesvonkamptz Design Associates (product design)

Forty thousand people live in the Märkisches Viertel in north Berlin, and a new wayfinding system was needed to help them find their way around. The design is visually sensitive and places emphasis on the key concepts of image, identity and function.

The system is based on two levels of information: pedestrians have their own footpaths, and drivers going through the quarter along a well-planned system of highways can easily see the directions en route.

Senftenberger Ring
↑ 18 20 22 24 26
← 28 30 32
→ 2 4 6 8 10
↑ Fußweg zum Atelier 24
18

Tall pylon: directions or general overview for the driver. This is the tallest pylon, and stands at the roadside. It has the largest font, so that it can easily be read as the driver goes by, and the same type of pylon with a complete map of the town and with information about the Märkisches Viertel has also been placed at ten key locations.

Middle-size pylon: This is for pedestrians. The viewing distance is considerably less, and so the pylon and the font are correspondingly smaller too. The pylon does not particularly stand out but simply blends in with the environment.

Low, curved pylon: This one displays a map of the district. It stands in places where additional wayfinding may be needed. The low level and the curve of the pylon make it easier for pedestrians and wheelchair users to read the map from a comfortable position.

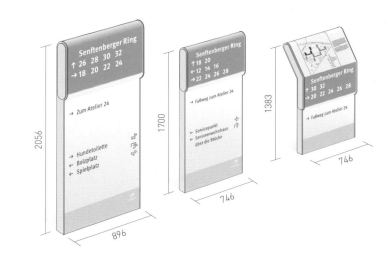

FGmq 78
TUeg 12

FF Meta and FF Meta Condensed,
Erik Spiekermann, 1991

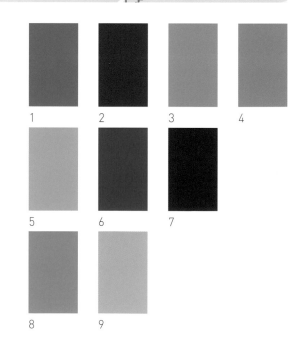

FF Meta is the house font of the Geso building. The narrower Meta Condensed was used for the signs.

A special group of pictograms was designed to supplement the typography, indicating individual items of information and depicting places unique to this quarter.

Owing to the layout of the Märkisches Viertel (winding roads and paths, large open areas in the centre), the streets need to be coded clearly. Each street is given its own colour, which makes for easier wayfinding within the district.

1 Senftenberger Ring
NSC S 0585-Y60R
2 Treuenbrietzener Straße
NSC S 3560-R
3 Quickborner Straße
NSC S 3050-B50G
4 Finsterwalder Straße
NSC S 0585-Y40R
5 Wilhelmsruher Damm
NSC S 0585-Y60R
6 Dannwalder Weg
NSC S 0585-Y60R
7 Tiefenseer Straße
NSC S 1080-G30Y
8 Wesendorfer Straße
NSC S 3060-G10Y
9 Eichhorster Weg
NSC S 2030-R80B

Public Spaces
Märkisches Viertel

Construction of the pylons: the head is made of Makrolon with 3M-film, and the body is aluminium. The lettering is on anti-graffiti 3M-film. The sides are aluminium, painted with ferric oxide.

Top curve

White lettering:
MetaCondBold-Roman 250 pt
Leading 306 pt
3M 3630-49

Lower curve

Grey lettering:
MetaCondBook-Roman 192 pt
Leading 255 pt
Colour: 3M 100-012

Base: screenprint
200 mm high
RAL-7011

The colour-coded, illuminated head displays the most important information: street name and house numbers. The aluminium section, immediately below, shows the next street and nearby locations. The light from above shines down on the additional information.

The back face of the pylon describes and explains the street names. In abstract form, it shows the special features of the places that have given the streets these names. Text-covered surfaces attract less graffiti.

Neckar Banks Development
Mannheim, Germany
1981
Stankowski + Duschek

Directly on the banks of the Neckar, this system provides a positive but fun formal language that helps residents and visitors alike. But even with such an original design, nothing can function effectively without the systematic allocation of information to different signs.

The whole complex and the site plan were divided into three sections. Signs for offshore high-rise and split-level houses were coded yellow, red and blue (primary colours) and given circular, square and triangular shapes (the most elementary geometrical forms). A timeless, neutral font and a square-based grid for information provide the simple basis. The high-rise buildings have a sign consisting of a yellow circle, a red triangle or a blue square, which makes it impossible to mix them up. The split-level houses have comparable codes, depending on their location. The underground car parks in these colour- and shape-coded areas feature fun pictures. Here too, everything is clearly readable, and each parking space has its identifying characteristic. Exits feature a stair graphic if there are stairs behind the doors, and all this information is conveyed without recourse to texts or individual words.

The intersection signs, where several arrow graphics come together, are attractive, with corresponding pictograms and bright colours. The same optimistic and animated design has been applied to notice boards and information signs.

The street signs are the most fun. Places such as the school, high-rises and river promenade are cut out in graphic form, and have clear typography.

Public Spaces
Neckar Banks Development

HLeag159

Helvetica 55 Roman,
Max Miedinger, 1957

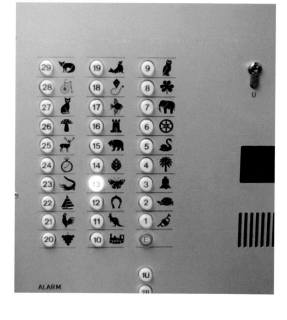

The different floors have symbols that children will recognize immediately, such as a cat or a clock. Children respond to pictures more readily because they find them easier than abstract numbers.

On each level, the symbols are repeated in colour and in large format, so that you know you're in the right place.

Dutch Street Signs
Netherlands
2002
npk industrial design
Gerard Unger (co-designer)

Following on from their successful design of four types of signpost for the Dutch ANWB – the equivalent of the British AA – npk were commissioned in 1998 to redesign the entire signage system (including symbols) of Dutch highways. The system, which was used at all intersections, was urgently in need of modernization, and it was essential to create signs that would meet the requirements of modern drivers and motorway maintenance workers.

The new system used a different font, reworked symbols and arrows (which went better with the new font) and a fresh layout. The new signs for main roads and motorways are more uniform, easier to read and therefore more efficient. All the changes and improvements were thoroughly tested at every stage by different bodies: the Dutch Organization for Applied Scientific Research (TNO) tested the new layout of the signs, and the consumer research group P5 Consultants checked that symbol comprehensibility met ISO 9186 standards.

The new signage system is clear and consistent: the old, arrow-shaped signs have been replaced by a rounder format with graphically well-defined arrows, and the symbols, font, directional arrows and road numbers are all perfectly integrated. The layout of information is the same on all the signs, and this too helps to create the clean, clear image envisaged by the ANWB.

Domburg

H De Roompot
Neeltje Jans

N 255

The new font was developed in collaboration with Gerard Unger. The letters are narrower, so that the signs are generally smaller but just as readable. The reduction in size meant a saving on materials, which greatly reduced the cost of the new system.

Public Spaces
Dutch Street Signs

Throughout the entire design process, great emphasis was laid on environmental aspects. After careful research, it was decided that the old supports, rather than being scrapped, should be re-used as the basis of the new system.

The new components are primarily made from durable materials such as high-grade steel and aluminium. Another important environmental consideration was energy consumption. By using energy-saving lights in conjunction with specially developed electronic equipment, the system cut electricity costs for the many thousands of street signs by around 50%.

PMS 102   PMS 032   PMS 300

Public Spaces
Dutch Street Signs

ABCDEFGHIJKLM
NOPQRSTUVWXYZ
abcdefghijklm
nopqrstuvwxyz
1234567890

ABCDEFGHIJKLMN
OPQRSTUVWXYZ
1234567890

Millennium Celebrations in Rome
Italy
2000
npk industrial design
Gerard Unger (co-designer)

The signage system was kept relatively simple, partly for technical reasons and production costs, but also to make it as user-friendly as possible for the millions of visitors.

The typeface stands in the unique, 2000-year-old tradition of ancient Roman public inscriptions. One of the many great merits of Roman antiquity was its lettering and range of beautiful capitals, especially the serif fonts. Rome was the birthplace of serif in its most perfect form, which continues to be used in so many languages, including Italian, English, French, German, Portuguese and Polish. It is equally effective both in large format, on signs that can be read from a distance, and in small format, on printed matter and screens.

PMS 130   PMS 485   PMS 349   PMS 661   PMS 5205

ABCDEFGHIJKLMNO
PQRSTUVWXYZÆŒ
abcdefghijklmnop
qrstuvwxyzæœ
0123456789 (.,-:;)

Capitolium,
Gerard Unger, 2000

This system of wayfinding and information based its colour scheme on characteristic Roman hues, taking walls and roofs, parks, historic sites and modern buildings as its inspiration – the rich, warm colours of southern Europe. Sometimes they were toned down, or combined with other colours.

Additional colours were only used when absolutely necessary, and even then they had to blend in harmoniously with the basic scheme. For some parts of the project and for special events, no particular colours were allocated, and so the designers were free to choose within the set parameters. The reds, yellows and blues have no connection with the typical primary colours of the Bauhaus and de Stijl. The yellow here is darker and more intense, while the red is more terra cotta. As there isn't a warm shade of blue, a fairly dark, rich tone was chosen. The green is warm and intense.

A series of arrows, symbols and pictograms was designed to complement the subtle details of the Capitolium font – for example, the elegant serifs, the contrast between the thick and thin strokes, and the gradual transition from one to the other. Instead of the rounded, oversimplified human figures normally used to indicate pedestrian zones and toilets, far more lifelike symbols were introduced. Godfather to these designs was one of the most impressive of all the ancient Roman arts – that of portraiture. The ancient Romans left for posterity a vast number of wonderfully abstract, stylized and yet astonishingly lifelike portraits.

These signs are as easy to read as modern, sans serif fonts. The details of the lettering have become so refined that they are suitable for nearly all our modern methods of reproduction. A few of the finer details have to be modified for use on screen, however – for example, the slightly curved form at the top or bottom of the serif appears straight, although the graphic character remains the same. Standard, italic and bold fonts are especially suitable for printed matter, and the light version works well on screen and in stone engraving.

The lettering is compact, with short upstrokes, downstrokes and thicker strokes in upper case. One design feature has been taken straight from antiquity – the calligraphic quality of many Roman inscriptions. All the letter forms are permeated by a movement from bottom left to top right, and are open and easy to read, whether in large or small format.

The design of this particular font, however, owes more to the early baroque versions in Giovanni Francesco Cresci's book *A Renaissance Alphabet* (*Il perfetto scrittore*) of 1571 than the original Roman model. This work contains suggestions for roman and italic font styles in lower case that fit in with the classical capitals.

There only two basic types of sign in three sizes: pedestrian signs in two sizes – 20 x 50 cm and 30 x 50 cm – and traffic signs of 30 x 110 cm.

All the signs have the same background colour: 70% Pantone 130. Texts and similar elements are in black. The top and bottom of the signs are bevelled, which is further reminiscent of chiselled inscriptions.

A sign – no, a signpost – can do more than just point towards a place. It can set the tone. It can give the place an identity. It can tell us something about the product, the people and the building. And if, as we read it, we forget about time and space, the system will quickly and politely direct us where we need to go.

BMW Plant Leipzig
Germany
2004
Moniteurs Gesellschaft für Kommunikationsdesign
GmbH (communications design)
Axel Kufus (product design)

In May 2005, this established car manufacturer started production at a new plant in Leipzig. The heart of the factory is the visionary central building. In Zaha Hadid's architectural design, the car bodies pass along non-stop conveyor belts above the heads of engineers, administrators and visitors, right through the transparent building to the various assembly points. In this way, every manager and employee is made permanently aware of the processes of production. This dynamic structure is echoed by the wayfinding system: inscribed bands of aluminium nestle up against the sculpted walls throughout this highly complex building. Up to 6 m in length, these so-called 'strings' reflect the formal language of the architecture and accompany the visitor through a veritable cascade of open spaces and structures.

The system comprises an intricate set of general plans, door plates and information boards. It provides a visual link between the central building and the workshops, and gives expression to the BMW philosophy that all departments share equally in the success of the company.

Part of the project was the detailed planning of a wayfinding system for the different factory buildings and the exterior of the 200-hectare site. More than 650 HGVs a day come off the assembly line of this Leipzig factory.

The company's house font, sans serif BMW, was used throughout the wayfinding and information system.

The signs and pictograms designed for the wayfinding system are also variations on the formal language of Zaha Hadid's architecture.

The signs are painted in subtly changing shades of blue-grey, which makes them seem more animated. The colour of the lettering and pictograms is a dark, easy-to-read sapphire blue.

The use of blue-grey tones underlies a system based on the length and layout of the different signs. The arrow on the directional signs, like the signs themselves, is directly related to the architectural forms.

The form of the directional sign acts as a signpost itself. The arrow shape at the end reinforces the direction of the sign.

AaBG 23

BMW Type, Bruno Maag

Non-recyclable waste

Food waste

Packaging materials

Waste paper

Sapphire blue, 3M film colour

NCS S 1510-R80B, matt

NCS S 1010-R80B, matt

NCS S 3010-R80B, matt

NCS S 2010-R80B, matt

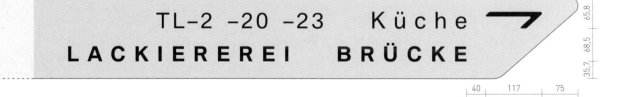

TL-2 -20 -23   Küche

LACKIEREREI   BRÜCKE

65,8
68,5
35,7

40   117   75

The top line of a directional 'string' shows the nearest locations in the order of their distance from the sign itself. The bottom line indicates the workshops and areas to be found at this particular point.

Businesses
BMW Plant Leipzig

General plans are
drawn in two sizes:
A3 landscape
(for fixed signs)
and 910 x 640 mm.
This template
can be reworked
and printed on the
premises.

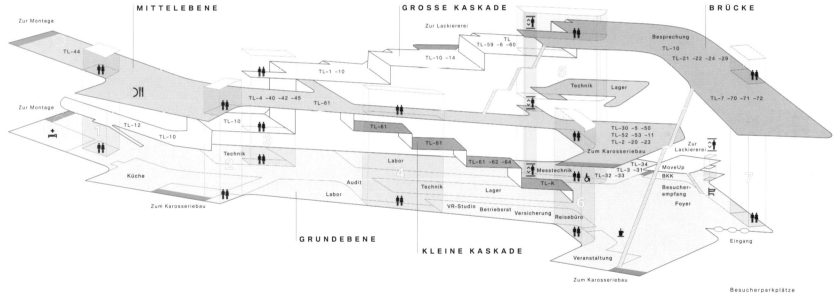

MITTELEBENE

GROSSE KASKADE

BRÜCKE

Zur Montage

Zur Lackiererei

Besprechung

TL-44

TL
TL-59 -6 -60

TL-10

TL-10 -14

TL-21 -22 -24 -29

TL-1 -10

Technik   Lager

Zur Montage

TL-4 -40 -42 -45   TL-61

TL-7 -70 -71 -72

TL-12

TL-10

TL-10

TL-61

TL-30 -5 -50
TL-52 -53 -11
TL-2 -20 -23

Technik

TL-61

Zum Karosseriebau

Zur
Lackiererei

Küche

Labor

TL-61 -62 -64   Messtechnik

TL-34
TL-3 -31
TL-32 -33

MoveUp

BKK

Zum Karosseriebau

Audit

Technik   Lager   TL-K

Besucher-
empfang

Foyer

Labor

VR-Studio Betriebsrat Versicherung Reisebüro

Eingang

GRUNDEBENE

KLEINE KASKADE

Veranstaltung

Zum Karosseriebau

Besucherparkplätze

BRÜCKE

TL-10
TL-21 -22 -24 -29   Besprechung Z37-Z77
TL-7 -70 -71 -72

KLEINE KASKADE

TL-K
TL-61 -62 -64

GROSSE KASKADE

TL-1 -10 -12 -14
TL-59
TL-6 -60

GRUNDEBENE

Audit   Messtechnik
Betriebsrat   MoveUp
Bistro   Reisebüro
BKK   Restaurant
Empfang   Shop
Foyer   Technik
Gesundheitsdienst   Veranstaltungsraum
Küche   Versicherung
Labor   VR-Studio
                     TL-3 -31 -32 -33 -34

MITTELEBENE

TL-11   Restaurant
TL-2 -20 -23
TL-4 -40 -42 -44 -45
TL-5 -50 -52 -53

● Standort

Depending on the amount of text, up to three directional signs can be placed one above another, with lengths of 2.5 m, 3 m, 4 m and 6 m. The juxtaposition of the signs varies according to the lengths.

Businesses
BMW Plant Leipzig

E.ON Main Administration Building
Munich, Germany
2004
büro uebele
visuelle kommunikation

E.ON Energie AG in Munich is one of the largest energy companies in Europe. The commission we were given was very limited: we had to design a signage system only for the offices. A conventional wayfinding system based, for example, on departments was ruled out for security reasons, and so the only course left open to us was to provide the offices with room identifications. That seemed inadequate to us, and we came up with a project that went beyond this limited scope but still complied with the client's wishes. We set ourselves the task of giving the whole place a graphic identity that would allow spontaneous wayfinding through the many buildings and sections, and derived the theme of our design from the work of the company itself – the production of energy. The German word *Strom*, meaning both 'current' and 'river', proved an apt starting-point and became our leitmotiv.

An aeon is an immeasurable length of time. Currents flow through space and time, and have done so for aeons. The word has its roots in the Latin *currere*, which means to run or flow. A river current is in a constant state of change, carving a path for itself as it flows through the countryside. Since the 18th century, electricity too has been flowing in currents, and this concept runs through all the different levels of the wayfinding system we designed for E.ON.

Hgle 023

→ →

Polo, Georg Salden, 1976
Arrows FF DIN,
Albert-Jan Pool, 1995

The house font is Polo, designed by Georg Salden. It's a very well-constructed font, with characteristic apertures and a striking lower-case 'g'. The Condensed style was used for the wayfinding system, as it takes up less space but is still just as easy to read. For typographical prioritization, the two styles Light and Strong were sufficient.

The arrows are taken from Albert-Jan Pool's FF DIN (1995). The two styles Regular and Bold correspond to the Light and Strong of Polo.

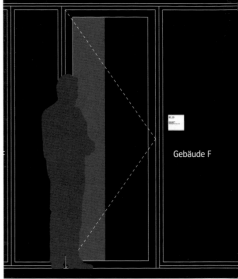

Silver

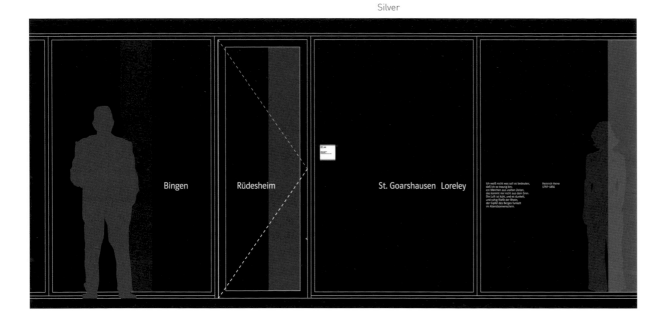

Bingen   Rüdesheim   St. Goarshausen Loreley   Gebäude F

Poetic Core
The five levels of the building are distinguished from one another through rivers. Places, landscapes, songs and poems give visual expression to the current.

Rivers flow through language areas, and this is a link with the international nature of the company, which produces electricity in different regions. Customers, visitors and workers may find their own hometown or country on one of the walls. The current takes on a visible form. Just like the references to towns and landscapes, stories and poems create associations that reinforce wayfinding. Which river is this? Visitors and workers may start talking to one another: 'I'm sitting below the Loreley!' Or they might go and see a colleague who is working in 'Vienna'.

Factual Information
On the walls opposite the rivers are directions that are easy to pick up on the move. They are repeated in such a way that they almost 'accompany' the visitor as he walks along – so he doesn't need to remember them. They tell him about the building, the level and the infrastructure, and how he can get to these areas.

The colours are like reflections on the water. Strips are clustered together like waterfalls on the transparent but reflective surfaces. The different sections of the buildings are given different colours, and the contrasts make it easier for people to find their way.

The colours are treated like sounds, with the musical score consisting of bright bands. These are composed like a sequence of notes, beside one another, below one another, and with pauses in between.

The colour itself is without body, but it throws its brightness over the walls and fittings. Each place is defined by its own individual and unmistakable atmosphere, and yet the atmosphere changes with the course of the sun.

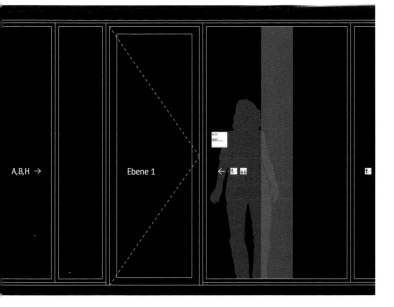

The motif of currents, visible on the different levels, is also developed in the colour concept. Each level and each section of the building is given different shades. The colours change from Level 1 to Level 5, and from south to north, and respectively from warm to cold. See also page 91.

The double glazing of the partition walls between offices is also used as a means of enriching the colour schemes. The coloured bands, which are screenprinted and transparent, are fixed alternately inside and outside the glass panes. As you move past them, there is an overlapping effect.

The office is a place in itself – defined by an imaginary current and by the bright light the colours lend to it.

The walls are covered with a silver web. These are graphic representations of the water as it changes with currents, wind and rain. The graphics have been cut from glossy reflective film, 1.2 mm thick, and stuck on the white partition walls of the offices.

Each of the five levels has its own graphics, which are seen on the interior partition walls. In order not to dazzle the eyes, the wave motifs are in negative form.

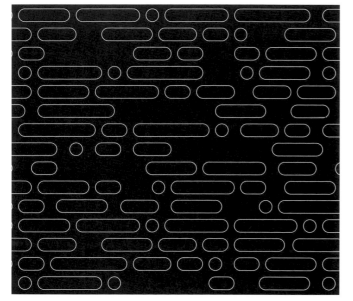

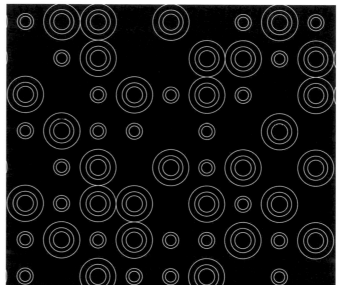

292

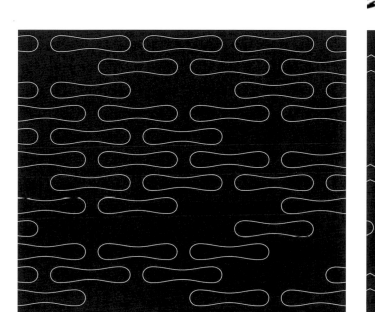

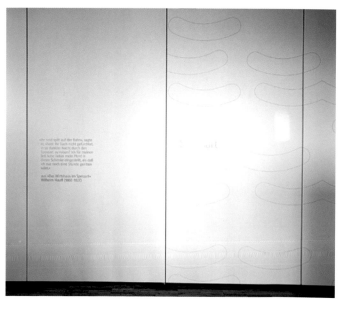

mediacampus
Zurich, Switzerland
2002
intégral ruedi baur zurich

The conditions for this project were rather unusual: just a few changes were made to the structure and the maintenance requirements of the site and buildings, with a view to temporary use over a period of about fifteen years. The idea of converting the site to a media campus came about during the dotcom boom. The redevelopment of the buildings had nothing to do with aesthetics, and everything to do with technology. The project's basic features – a high-performance data network – remained invisible in terms of the technical infrastructure. The site of the former printing works became a digital data platform, the buildings became the modules, and the floor became the circuit board. For the most part the project consisted of showing the outside world the changes in and the revaluation of this otherwise unprepossessing building through simple means that fitted in with the urban context. The system also provided wayfinding through the site and the buildings.

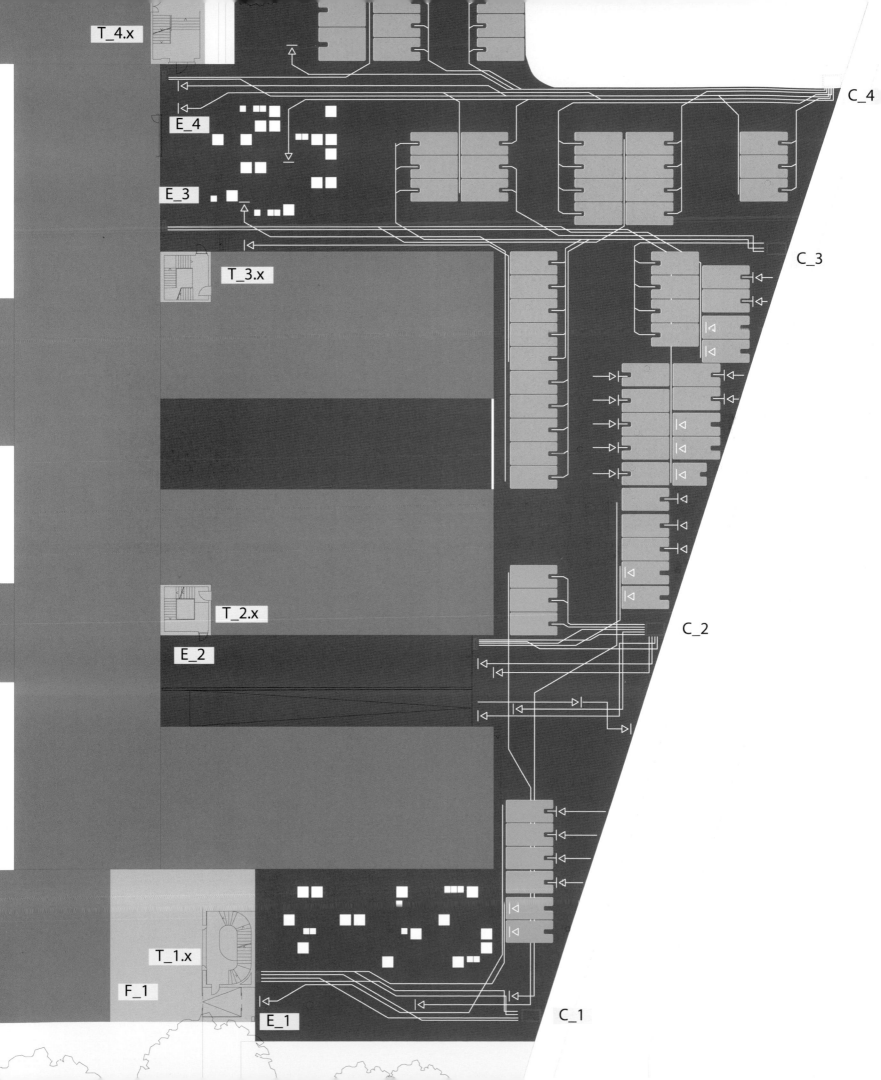

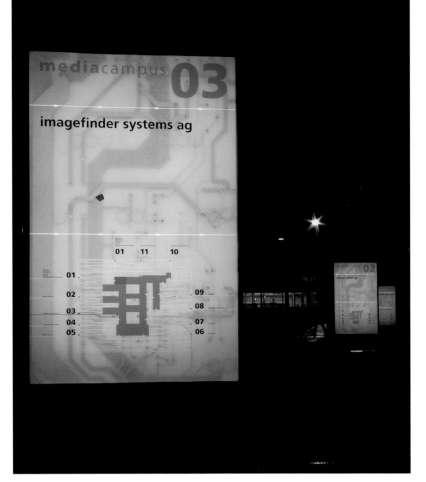

Throughout the day, the area is marked out by coloured pieces of micro-architecture, like oversized boundary stones. At night, the internally illuminated signs shine out into the cityscape. The aesthetic appearance, themes and colours all denote the new use of the complex. These containers consist of a base of exposed concrete, supporting a structure of steel and glass.

The colourful circuit-board motifs and all the permanent information signs are printed digitally, and pasted onto the backs of the glass panes. Temporary information is printed on film and stuck to the front of the glass.

Additional constructions to support the flaps

Side panels of chrome steel, diam. = c. 5 mm

Side panel can be opened in order to make changes

Base: readymade exposed concrete; surface smooth-formed finish with smallest possible chamfer, max. 5 mm. Open bottom for drainage and ventilation.

Lighting: fluorescent, dimmable, can be used outside and in damp conditions

The light intensity can be adjusted according to the degree of daylight through light gauges in the container

Graphics: held by ESG glass, diam. = 10 mm, attached to steel tube frame

Construction: steel tube frame with square edges, 50 x 50 x 2.5 mm

285

60

200

130

01.1 | 001

mediacampus **01**

1.
↳ genossenschaft
mediacampus
↳ svox ag
↳ streamlx ag
↳ aseantic ag
↳ edumaag
↳ haustechnik

The colour layout distinguishes between the colourful exterior and the more restrained interior. Indoors, the wayfinding system blends in with the existing architecture. Information points are defined on wall surfaces but do not encroach: a change in the plaster and a higher degree of gloss in the colours are all that distinguish them from the plain background. In keeping with the internal architecture, the degree of colour is reduced, with the backgrounds remaining matt white for the roughcast and glossy for the communications surfaces. Permanent lettering is stencilled, while temporary information is on film. The latter is limited to grey and black to distinguish it.

iA Rb 05

The client's existing house font was Frutiger, and the styles used were Frutiger LT Bold and Frutiger LT Black.

DGF STOESS AG
Eberbach, Germany
2003
büro uebele
visuelle kommunikation

DGF STOESS AG is a market leader in the production of gelatin. The gelatin manufacturing process is given visual expression and displayed on the five levels of the building. The graphics that have been used represent horizontal and vertical sections of molecules and chemicals before and during heating.

Places and directions: The building is criss-crossed with routes indicated with marker 'stones'. These stones indicate and point out specific locations, uniting form and structure. The marking of places with stones is a tried and trusted technique, and traces of it can be seen in local place names such as Königstein, Kreuzberg, Steinbrunnen. Each 'Stein' [stone] is a cuboid or hexahedron, the five visible sides of which contain different combinations of text, colour and pattern. The changes in light and shade around these cuboids are reinforced by changes in colour, with a horizontal face in black placed next to a vertical one in grey.

Pitch and tone: The colours are a continuation of the achromatic architectural design. The colour scheme is taken from the building materials, the dominant one being red limestone. This was then developed by extending the basic red towards yellow and white, giving rise to a dominant harmony of reds with overtones of pink and orange.

Building molecules: The production of gelatin is illustrated as if stroboscopically, with the basic images built up into graphic patterns, which vary according to their positioning. The colours follow horizontal and vertical motion through the building, with the graphics superimposed on top. At points of intersection, a menhir-like arrangement of several stones is created, each with its own unmistakable colour and design.

The typographical elements on the cubes are varied within the grid, in order to avoid a repetition of combinations. The arrows and numbers are made from white transfer tape. Font size: 51.5 pt, arrow size: 217.5 pt.

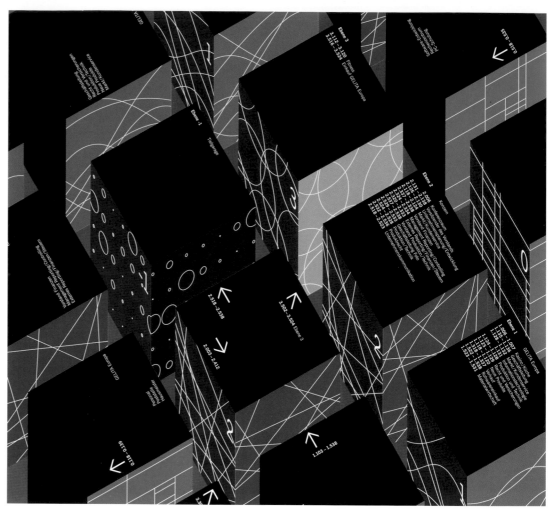

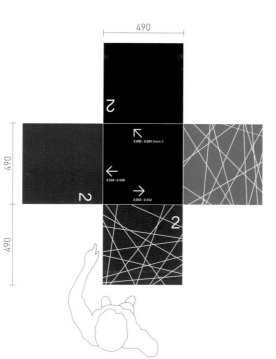

The reading direction on the top face is always from the observer's point of view, which means that his standpoint has to be determined in advance. There are two patterned faces: the first, which is coloured, always faces towards the main entrance and does not contain any indication of the floor level; the second, immediately adjacent, designates the floor level. This side always has the colour NCS S 7500-n, and faces the main flow of people. The next side is also NCS S 7500-n, but has no pattern. The fourth side and the top are coloured with NCS S 8500-n. The lines of the patterns are 0.55 mm thick.

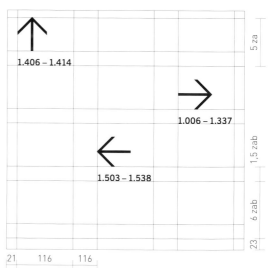

Antique pink RAL 3015
Level 1

Signal orange RAL 2010
Level 2

Light pink RAL 3014
Level 3

Yellow orange RAL 2000
Level 0

Orient red RAL 3031
Level -1

NCS S
7500-n

NCS S
8500-n

Floor   Room

2.119

Area

Pbkj
456

→

→

News Gothic and
News Gothic Bold,
Morris Fuller Benton, 1908

FF DIN Regular and Bold

The floors are numbered from -1 (underground car park) through 0 (ground floor) to 3. The different levels are divided into five areas, beginning with the figure 0 (entrance hall, canteen etc). This division of the building has the advantage of giving the same final number to rooms directly above one another and serving the same purpose – for instance, kitchenettes.

This is clearly an aid to wayfinding. Room numbers, like house numbers, are divided up between odd and even, with odd numbers in ascending order on the left, and even in ascending order on the right.

News Gothic, designed by Morris Fuller Benton in 1908, is a tried and tested font. It is narrow, and therefore ideal for wayfinding systems in which a great deal of information has to be displayed in a small space. It is one of a series of American sans serif fonts. Despite the narrowness of its linear cut, it has distinctly different thicknesses of stroke.

Linear-Antiqua is a plainer font, but is nevertheless individual and easy on the eye. Combination font/arrow: News Gothic Bold/ FF DIN Bold, and News Gothic Roman/FF DIN Regular.

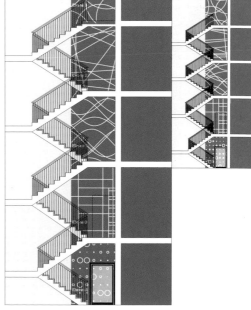

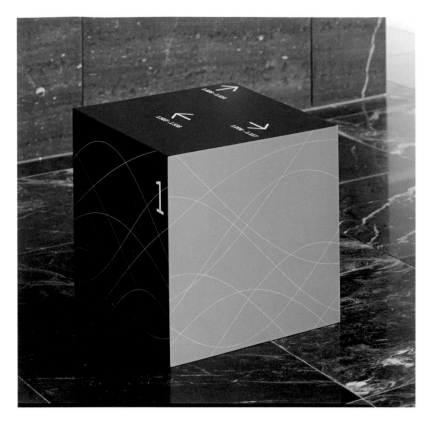

Below: View through
the entrance doors
of the foyer, showing
several cubes. The
patterns on the glass
doors superimpose
themselves on the
cube patterns,
creating a rich,
three-dimensional
graphic image.

Below: Graphic
design can help to
give particular rooms
– like the fitness
centre illustrated
here, or kitchenette –
a special identity of
their own.

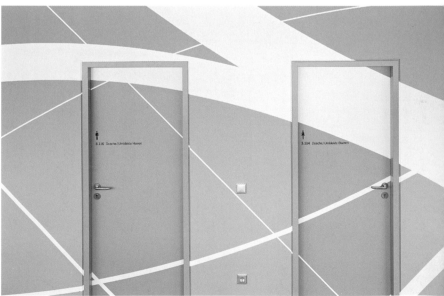

Businesses
DGF STOESS AG

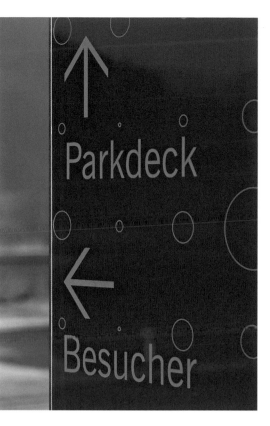

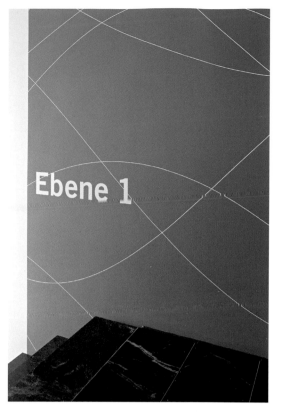

Above: Outside the building are free-standing signs without frames, made of multilayer glass with two-colour glass-ceramic screenprint between the layers.

Below: The patterns constitute a graphic programme that can be developed and used for different purposes. The world map in the foyer is the pride of any international company, and this too is visualized in terms of the design of the ground floor.

Above: Staircase with gelatin patterns. The walls are partially painted with one colour from the system, and the large-format, symmetrical negative pattern is applied to the surface with transfer tape. The sweeping white lines are 2.5 mm thick.

Zürcher Kantonalbank
Steinfels Administration Building
Zurich, Switzerland
2004
intégral ruedi baur zurich

For the interior of the new Steinfels administration building in Zurich, a signage system was designed to combine the functions of identification, wayfinding and atmosphere.

The conventional problems of wayfinding were less pronounced here than in many other such projects owing to the strict rationality of the architecture. The interior layout of the building gives natural guidance. The signage system therefore had to strike a fine balance – making its presence felt, while at the same time remaining as unobtrusive as possible, in harmony with the architecture.

The artist Bruno Nagel collaborated on a typographical design for the central foyer of the 'Steinfels' which gave the rooms an individual identity and also established a dialogue between the different levels and sections of the building. By giving each façade and room a name, the architecture takes on a new, poetic dimension. Bruno Nagel's words give the spaces their own identity and make it possible to describe areas and workplaces in verbal terms.

Sha**12**

Futura Book and Bold,
Paul Renner, 1928

A8p

UHF, Yuji Adachi, 1999

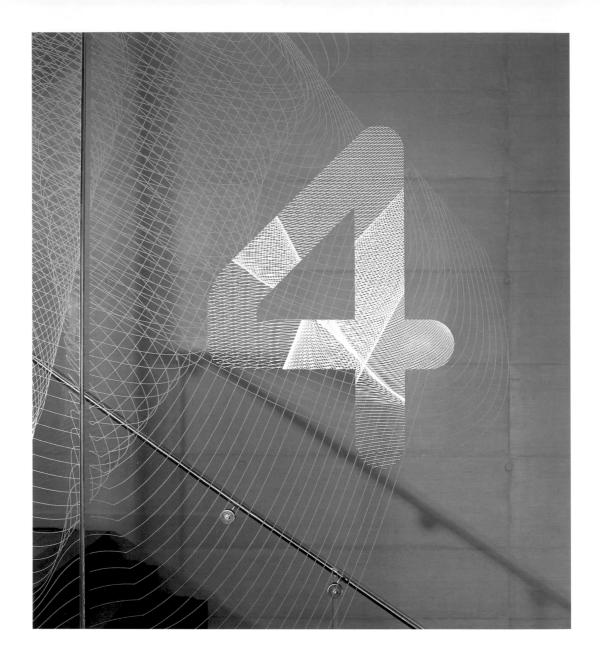

The client's existing house font – Futura, in the styles of Book and Bold – was used for primary lettering, and the monospace font UHF for secondary. The arrows are equilateral triangles that have also been developed from Futura.

General sign at the entrance:
Numbers: 820/851 pt,
Text: 130/170 pt.
Lift numbers: 200 pt,
Text: 032/042 pt.
Floor level numbers:
500 pt, text: 184/236 pt.
Department entrances – text: 184/236 pt.
Doors to departments and side rooms – text: 130/170 pt.

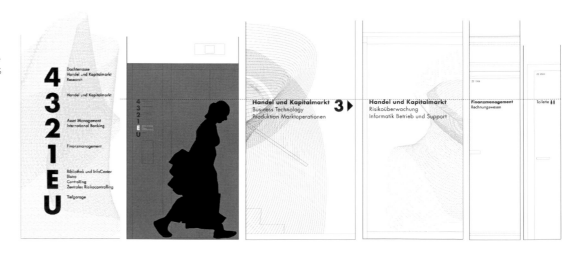

Businesses
Zürcher Kantonalbank

Handel und Kapitalmarkt

The typography and graphics distinguish between primary and secondary information.

The primary signage system has the function of opening up the different sections of the building and the underground car park. This is supplemented by a secondary, associative system in the main foyer.

Information in the primary system is separated into foreground and background. The foreground conveys the necessary directional information, while the linear graphics in the background subtly cancel out the transparency of the glass. With fixed glass installations and sliding doors, the so-called guilloche lines prevent accidents.

For the secondary system, the texts are significantly larger. Foreground and background are typographically merged. Text and guilloche lines together show up the transparency of the glass. The graphics, in addition to fulfilling the function of identification, also provide protection for people in the adjacent offices.

HypoVereinsbank Executive Offices
Munich, Germany
2005
büro uebele
visuelle kommunikation

This whole building sends out the message 'This place is private.' Visitors are received here as guests, politely accompanied by their host to the dining-room, through the library, and finally back to the exit. It would never occur to anyone to allow the guest to wander alone through this building. Directions on the walls would create an impression of openness to the public and, in this respect, of impersonality.

The buildings date from the 17th and 19th centuries, and have a quiet, discreet charm. The board of directors and management committee have their offices on the top floor, and on the lower levels there are rooms for different events. Here too, visitors are given a personal welcome, although not by any person. The wayfinding system takes over this function, assuming the role of the deferential servant.

The language of the graphics is soft and respectful. The information accompanies the visitor without his having to look for it, because it lies quite literally at his feet. There are no boards or other extraneous constructions to disturb the gentle harmony of the architecture. The glittering signs of terrazzo and granite are inlaid in the floor, and blend in naturally and confidently with the spaces.

The letters are made of burnished high-grade steel. A precise negative form was stuck on the floor with transfer tape as a stencil, and then cut out of the terrazzo with sandblasting. The letters, pictograms and arrows were fitted precisely, within a few hundredths of a millimetre, into these sunken, negative forms without any visible join.

Information accompanies the visitor on his way through the building. The discreet signage system pays full respect to the architecture, providing all the directions necessary, but never forcing itself into the foreground.

Businesses
HypoVereinsbank Executive Offices

The large lettering on the left shows where you are now, and the smaller lettering on the right indicates the direction you should take. The signs reflect the sky and the colours of the building.

Hgax
239

Frutiger 75 Black,
Adrian Frutiger, 1976
House font for the HVB Group

Arrow: FF DIN Black,
Albert-Jan Pool, 1995

The principle of
discreet signage
is also applied
consistently in the
different entrances.
Identifications
are inlaid in the
pavements outside.

The removable door
labels are made with
a special transfer
tape, screenprinted
in silver. The adhesive
keeps the lettering in
place, but individual
letters can easily be
removed.

Businesses
HypoVereinsbank Executive Offices

1.03.004 Jungfernturm

Silver

High-grade
polished
steel

The silver lettering on walls and doors echoes the reflective metal letters. The achromatic nature of these silver signs blends in with the restrained colours of the architecture as well as with the high-grade steel handrails and door handles.

The burnished steel letters reflect the light, and as the sun moves across the sky, the words move across the walls.

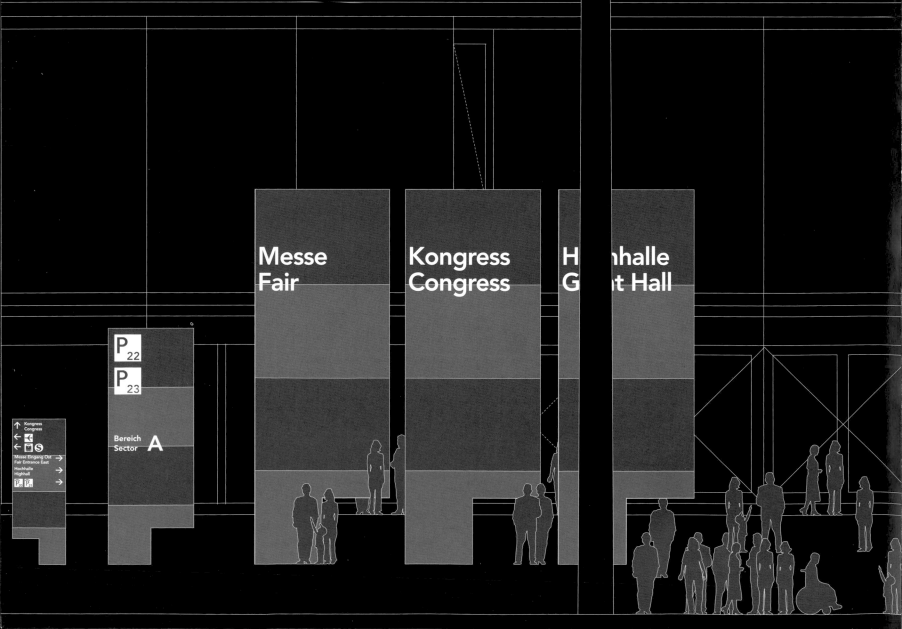

A multilingual hubbub, a colourful sound, a confusion of voices and a concert of colours. The visitor's mood is set for conviviality, for contact with countless colleagues, for something new. The system guides him to the right place, taking him by the hand so that he will not get lost in the maelstrom. And though the way may be long, it's entertaining: you see a ballet of balloons, rainbow-striped signs, and shining letters in the ground. Where was it that you wanted to go?

Brooklyn Academy of Music (BAM)
New York, USA
1997–2006
Pentagram Design, New York

The Brooklyn Academy of Music is the oldest centre for the performing arts in the USA today. In 1995, a graphic wayfinding system was developed for the BAM Next Wave Festival, the annual highlight of the cultural calendar. The designers decided on partially hidden signs to give the impression of something 'appearing on the horizon' – a visual metaphor that illustrates the focus of these Next Wave festivals as a showcase for young talent. The concept proved to be such a success that it was taken over for all other events at the BAM, and ultimately became a feature of the institution's identity. In the meantime, the BAM Local Development Corporation (LDC) has begun to redesign the whole BAM complex and its surroundings as a cultural centre. A rather old free-standing sign on Flatbush Avenue was given a makeover, and now after years of disuse it points proudly to the BAM area, advertising the daily programme of events that take place there. On its mast, the letters BAM rotate – the movement underlining the dynamic revival of the complex, and also ensuring that people on both sides of Flatbush Avenue can see the letters BAM loud and clear.

Culture, Congresses and Trade Fairs

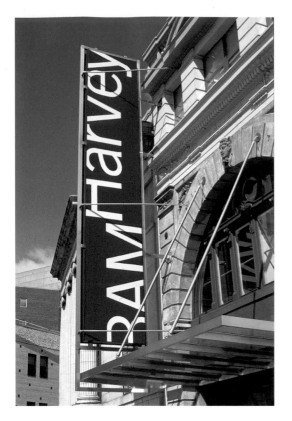

BAM Harvey Theater

The graphic designers were commissioned to work with the architect Hugh Hardy on renovating the BAM opera house. Among the tasks involved were the installation of a lift and the construction of various new areas for visitors, including a lobby on the mezzanine floor and cinemas. The designers produced signs for indoors and out, information stands, a founder's plaque, and also a new façade for another venue – the BAM Harvey Theater. The redevelopment of the old, historic BAM was used as an opportunity to spread the new BAM image through all the buildings, and this was incorporated into all the new signs. The signage programme was another important step towards the creation of a large-scale, integrated BAM experience for the crowds of enthusiastic visitors.

Culture, Congresses and Trade Fairs
Brooklyn Academy of Music

The white balloons with red lettering not only provided clear signs but were also a striking symbol of the event. When the congress was over, the balloons were given away to the employees or to children. The paper signs suspended from the balloons were easy to change, and they kept visitors informed about all the current items on the programme.

Culture, Congresses and Trade Fairs
Icograda Congress

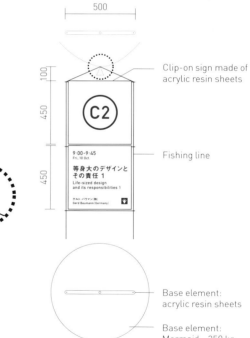

Clip-on sign made of
acrylic resin sheets

Fishing line

Base element:
acrylic resin sheets

Base element:
Mermaid – 350 kg
diam. = 700-20
punched plate

eiC 145+

FF DIN Medium,
Albert-Jan Pool, 1995

100M 100Y
10K

New 42nd Street Studios/Duke Theater
New York, USA
2000
Pentagram Design, New York

The New 42nd Street Studios are on 42nd Street in New York, between Broadway and 8th Avenue. The building was designed for the contractor, New 42nd Street, by Charles Platt of Platt Byard Dovell White Architects. The ten-storey complex houses rehearsal rooms for performing artists and the Duke Theater, which seats 199 people.

The wayfinding system was designed to fit in with the architecture and the uses of the building. The designers saw the building as a kind of factory for artists. The lettering is influenced by de Stijl and modern Dutch fonts, and the idea of placing directions on the floor came from the strips of adhesive that are used to mark the positions of performers on the stage and the concert platform. The fixing of the signs (and the founder's plaque in etched plate glass) is quite conventional, but it reflects the excitement of live performances and also the profusion of illuminated advertisements in nearby Times Square. The materials used inside the building were acrylic, aluminium, photopolymer, perforated metal, linoleum and paint.

Throughout the building, giant-sized letters and numbers form directions that fill the narrow corridors and guide visitors to the different rooms and floors. The signs are laser-cut from robust vinyl, set in the floor, and sometimes continued on the walls.

The floors of the lifts bear the word 'floor'. When the lift door opens, the number of that floor lies directly in front of it.

StBe 03

FB Agency,
(Morris Fuller Benton, 1933)
David Berlow, 1989

Culture, Congresses and Trade Fairs
New 42nd Street Studios/Duke Theater

'We got lost...and with my topography I had to help find the way....' Johann Gottfried Seume

Zürcher Kantonalbank, Steinfels
Administration Building, Zurich,
Switzerland, 2004
Communications design: intégral
ruedi baur zurich Project leader:
Ruedi Baur, Axel Steinberger
Team: Jürgen X. Albrecht, Aline
Ledergerber, Bruno Nagel,
Jana Strozinsky Client: Zürcher
Kantonalbank ZKB Architect: Kuhn
Fischer Partner Architekten, Zurich
Graphic work: Eicher Werkstätten
Photos: Andreas Körner Pages
304–7

Bureaus

**Adler & Schmidt GmbH
Kommunikations-Design**
Pfalzburger Straße 43–44
10717 Berlin, Germany
T +49.30.86 00 07-0
F +49.30.86 00 07-20
kontakt@adler-schmidt.de
www.adler-schmidt.de

BaseBRU
Chaussée de Forest 62
1060 Brussels, Belgium
T +32.2.2 19 00 82
F +32.2.2 29 31 60
basebru@basedesign.com
www.basedesign.com

BaseNYC
Lafayette 158, 5th Floor
New York, NY 10013, USA
T +1.2 12.6 25 92 93
F +1.2 12.6 25 02 32
basenyc@basedesign.com
www.basedesign.com

Braun Engels Gestaltung
Judenhof 11
89073 Ulm, Germany
T +49.7 31.6 38 62
F +49.7 31.6 38 63
braun@braun-engels.de
www.braun-engels.de

Bruce Mau Design Inc.
197 Spadina Avenue, Suite 501
Toronto, Ontario
Canada M5T 2C8
T +1. 4 16.2 60-57 77
F +1. 4 16.2 60-27 70
studio@brucemaudesign.com
www.brucemaudesign.com

Bureau Mijksenaar
Paasheuvelweg 20
1105 BJ Amsterdam
The Netherlands
T +31.0.20.691 47 29
F +31.0.20.409 02 44
office@mijksenaar.com
www.mijksenaar.com

**büro uebele
visuelle kommunikation**
Heusteigstraße 94a
70180 Stuttgart, Germany
T +49.7 11.34 17 02-0
F +49.7 11.34 17 02-30
info@uebele.com
www.uebele.com

Designgruppe Flath & Frank
Haimhauserstraße 4
80802 Munich, Germany
T +49.89.33 05 67-0
F +49.89.33 05 67-28
office@designgruppe.de
www.designgruppe.de

Gottschalk & Ash Toronto
113 Dupont St., Suite 103
Toronto, Ontario
Canada M5R 1V4
T +1.4 16.9 63-97 17
F +1.4 16.9 63-93 51
info@gplusa.com
www.gplusa.com

**Gourdin & Müller
Büro für Gestaltung**
Fichtestraße 7
04275 Leipzig, Germany
T +49.34.13 01 91 15
F +49.34.12 31 94 41
info@gourdin-mueller.de
www.gourdin-mueller.de

Hiromura Design Office Inc.
MAK Flat 6F, 6-11-8
Minamiaoyama,
Minato-ku, Tokyo 107-0062
Japan
T +81.3.34 09-55 46
F +81.3.34 09-55 72

intégral ruedi baur et associés
5, Rue Jules Vallès,
75011 Paris
France
T + 33.1.55 25 81 10
F +33.1.43 48 08 07
atelier@integral.ruedi-baur.com
www.integral.ruedi-baur.com

intégral ruedi baur zurich
Kleinstrasse 16
8008 Zurich
Switzerland
T +41.43.2 68 41 91
F +41.43.2 68 41 93
zrh@irb-zuerich.ch

KMS Team GmbH
Deroystraße 3–5
80335 Munich, Germany
T +49.89.49 04 11-0
F +49.89.49 04 11-49
info@kms-team.de
www.kms-team.de

MetaDesign AG
Leibnizstraße 65
10629 Berlin, Germany
T +49.30.59 00 54-0
F +49.30.59 00 54-111
mail@metadesign.de
www.metadesign.de

**moniteurs
Gesellschaft für
Kommunikationsdesign GmbH**
Ackerstraße 21
10115 Berlin, Germany
T +49.30.24 34 56-0
F +49.30.24 34 56-56
info@moniteurs.de
www.moniteurs.de

n|p|k industrial design bv
Noordeinde 2d
2311 CD Leiden
The Netherlands
T +31.71.5 14 13 41
F +31.71.5 13 04 10
npk@npk.nl
www.npk.nl

Pentagram Design Ltd.
Leibnizstraße 60
10629 Berlin, Germany
T +49.30.2 78 76 10
F +49.30.27 87 61 10
info@pentagram.de
www.pentagram.de

Pentagram
204 Fifth Avenue
New York, NY 10010
USA
T +1.2 12.6 83 70 00
F +1.2 12.5 32 01 81
info@pentagram.com
www.pentagram.com

**Polyform
Büro für Grafik- und
Produktdesign**
Brunnenstraße 196
10119 Berlin, Germany
T +49.30.28 04 97 90
F +49.30.28 04 97 99
info@polyform-net.de
www.polyform-net.de

Stankowski + Duschek
Grafisches Atelier
Lenbachstraße 43
70192 Stuttgart, Germany
T +49.711.89 66 45-0
F +49.711.89 66 45-11
atelier@st-du.de
www.st-du.de

Total Identity
Niederlassung Amsterdam
Paalbergweg 42
1105 BV Amsterdam ZO
Postbus 12480
1100 AL Amsterdam ZO
The Netherlands
T +31.20.7 50 95 00
F +31.20.7 50 95 01
info@totalidentity.nl
www.totalidentity.nl

333

Bibliography

Rayan Abdullah, Roger Hübner: *Pictograms, Icons & Signs: A Guide to Information Graphics*, London: Thames & Hudson, 2006

Otl Aicher, *Analogous and Digital*, Berlin: Ernst & Sohn Verlag, 1994

Otl Aicher, *Gehen in der Wüste*, Frankfurt: S. Fischer Verlag, 1982

Otl Aicher, *Martin Krampen: Zeichensysteme der visuellen Kommunikation*, Berlin: Ernst & Sohn Verlag, 1996

Otl Aicher, *The World as Design*, translated by Michael Robinson, Berlin: Ernst & Sohn Verlag, *c*. 1994

Akita Design Kan, *The Dude Says*, Tokyo: Akita Design Kan, 2001

Prof. Dr Hermann von Baravalle, *Geometrie als Sprache der Formen*, Stuttgart: Verlag Freies Geistesleben, 1963

Baumann & Baumann, *lechts rinks, Orientierungen zwischen Architektur und Parlament*, Stuttgart: Hatje Cantz Verlag, 1995

Baumann & Baumann, *Spiel Räume*, Stuttgart: Hatje Cantz Verlag, 2002

Bertron & Schwarz, *RaumZeitZeichen Transmediale Projekte*, Mainz: Verlag Hermann Schmidt Mainz, 1999

Hartmut Brückner, *Informationen gestalten*, Bremen: Verlag H. M. Hauschild, 2004

Thierry Brunfaut, Juliette Cavanaile, *Basebook 2*, Barcelona: Actar, 2004

Büro für Gestaltung Wangler & Abele, *gestalten eins, zwei*, Munich: Büro für Gestaltung Wangler & Abele, 2002

Roger Fawcett-Tang, *Mapping: An Illustrated Guide to Graphic Navigational Systems*, East Sussex: RotoVision, 2002

Friedrich Forssman, Ralf de Jong, *Detailtypografie*, Mainz: Verlag Hermann Schmidt Mainz, 2002

Adrian Frutiger, *Eine Typografie*, Solothurn: Vogt-Schild-Verlag, 1995

Ulrike Gauss, Stankowski Foundation, *Stankowski 06 Aspekte des Gesamtwerks*, Stuttgart: Hatje Cantz Verlag, 2006

Walter Herdeg (ed.): *archigraphia: architektur- und signalisierungsgraphik*, Zurich: Graphis Press Zürich, 1978

Martin Hess, *formvollendet eine sammlung ästhetischer mathematisch definierter formen*, Sulgen|Zurich: Verlag Niggli AG, 2005

Institute for Information Design, *Information Design Source Book*, Basel: Birkhäuser Verlag, 2005

intégral ruedi baur et associés, *Constructions*, Baden: Lars Müller Publishers, 1998

intégral ruedi baur et associés, *Identité visuelle du Centre Pompidou*, Paris: Jean-Michel Place, 2000

Immanuel Kant, *Kant: Political Writings*, H. Reiss (ed.), translated by H. B. Nisbet, Cambridge: Cambridge University Press, 1990

Herbert W. Kapitzki, *Herbert W. Kapitzki. Design: Method and Consequence. A Biographical Report*, London & Stuttgart: Edition Axel Menges, 1997

Christian Lutsch, Heinz-Peter Lahaye, *Orientierung Standpunkte: Orientierung in Gesellschaft, Wissenschaft und Medien*, Stuttgart: Hatje Cantz Verlag, 2003

Gerhard Mack, *Rémy Zaugg: une Monographie*, Luxembourg: Fondation Mudam, 2005

Hiromura Masaaki, *Space Graphysm*, Amsterdam: BIS Publishers, 2003

Philipp Meuser, Daniela Pogade, *Raumzeichen: Architektur und Kommunikations·Design*, Berlin: DOM publishers, 2005

Per Mollerup, *Wayshowing: A Guide to Environmental Signage Principles and Practices*, Baden: Lars Müller Publishers, 2005

Pentagram: The Compendium, London: Phaidon Press, 1993

Arthur Rüegg, *Polychromie architecturale*, Basel: Birkhäuser Verlag, 1997

Anton Stankowski, *Das Gesamtwerk 1925–1982*, Stuttgart: Verlag Gerd Hatje, 1983

Stankowski + Duschek, *Der Pfeil: Gestalt und Ziel*, Stuttgart: Wilhelm Verlag, 1985

Jan Tschichold, *Schriften 1925–1974 Vols 1 + 2*, Berlin: Verlag Brinkmann & Bose, 1991

Edward R. Tufte, *Envisioning Information*, Cheshire: Graphics Press, 1990

Edward R. Tufte, *The Visual Display of Quantitative Information*, Cheshire: Graphics Press, 1983

Edward R. Tufte, *Visual Explanations*, Cheshire: Graphics Press, 1997

Andreas Uebele, *schrift im raum*, Mainz: Verlag Hermann Schmidt Mainz, 1999

Andreas Uebele, *weg zeichen/ my type of place*, Mainz: Verlag Hermann Schmidt Mainz, 2003

Why not Associates, *Why not Associates? 2: Graphic Design, Film and Photography*, London: Thames & Hudson, 2004

Peter Wildbur, Michael Burke, *Information Graphics: Innovative Solutions in Contemporary Design*, London: Thames & Hudson, 1999

Susan Yelavich (ed.), *Profile: Pentagram Design*, London: Phaidon Press, 2004

Moritz Zwimpfer, *2D Visual Perception: Elementary Phenomena of Two-dimensional Perception. A Handbook for Artists and Designers*, Sulgen|Zurich: Verlag Niggli AG, 1994

Moritz Zwimpfer, *Colour, Light, Sight, Sense: An Elementary Theory of Colour in Pictures*, West Chester, PA: Schiffer, *c*. 1988

Moritz Zwimpfer, *Visuelle Wahrnehmung*, Sulgen|Zurich: Verlag Niggli AG, 1994

Index

Translated from the German *Orientierungssysteme und Signaletik* by David H. Wilson

First published in the United Kingdom in 2007 by
Thames & Hudson Ltd, 181A High Holborn,
London WC1V 7QX

www.thamesandhudson.com

First published in 2007 in hardcover in the
United States of America by Thames & Hudson Inc.,
500 Fifth Avenue, New York, New York 10110

thamesandhudsonusa.com

Original edition © 2006 Andreas Uebele and
Verlag Hermann Schmidt Mainz, Mainz

This edition © 2007 Thames & Hudson Ltd, London

British Library Cataloguing-in-Publication Data
A catalogue record for this book is available from the
British Library

Library of Congress Catalog Card Number 2007922779

ISBN 978-0-500-51379-8   348317

Printed in China

741.6 UEB